LIVING
for
GOD

SEVEN PILLARS TO A VIRTUOUS LIFESTYLE

LIVING for GOD

ARMENTA HOWERTON

ISBN: 979-8-89031-387-4 (sc)
ISBN: 979-8-89031-388-1 (hc)
ISBN: 979-8-89031-389-8 (e)

Library of Congress Control Number: 2020924062

One Galleria Blvd., Suite 1900, Metairie, LA 70001
1-888-421-2397

But I did find this: God created people to be virtuous, but they have each turned to follow their own downward path.

—Ecclesiastes 7:29 NLT

Contents

Foreword

To be virtuous means you have conformed your life to fit the mold of moral and ethical uprightness. You have aligned yourself with the purpose, preciseness, and exactitude of God, and you live according to His precepts and statues to reflect His glory in the earth.

> His divine power has granted to us all things that pertain to life and godliness, through the knowledge of him who called us to his own glory and excellence, by which he has granted to us his precious and very great promises, so that through them you may become partakers of the divine nature, having escaped from the corruption that is in the world because of sinful desire. For this very reason make every effort to supplement your faith with virtue, and virtue with knowledge. (2 Peter 1:3–5 ESV)

Second Peter 1:3–5 reminds us that He has given us power through the knowledge of His Word, that through His promises we can escape moral decay, which is in the world, in order to become partakers of His divine nature. It also admonishes us to work diligently in every area possible to build a disposition that shapes our intent and expresses his characteristics as a holy God. Min. Armenta Howerton has developed a practical manual that probes deeply into the heart of the relationship with the Father and creates understanding that equips us to live a virtuous lifestyle. It is impossible to function as agents of change if we don't understand, apply, and operate through faith in these seven pillars. When we know the tools and their specific purpose, we can develop strategy at the core level and have a settled approach to living in him so that our character and integrity speaks well of him. Virtuous living properly positions us to serve the body as living epistles. Society's jaded perspective of faith requires us to be the very change we want to see, for words without deeds are as meaningless as seeds blowing in the wind. These pillars plant the seeds of foundation, which will support the reconstruction process of our inner man that will outwardly speak through our lives. In her obedience Min. Howerton has offered us pertinent reminders that reveal the roots of a purposeful relationship with the Father, which in turn reveals his purposes and power here in the earth. This is a crucial time for believers because the winds of change are moving so violently in this final dispensation. Our foundation in him must be sure so we don't waver, falter, or fall out of the faith. Thank you, Min. Howerton, for your obedience to the call so that our hearts and minds can be grounded in him.

Min. Amanda F. Standard,
Founder and Artistic Director
Divine Dance Institute, Inc.

Preface

Not long after answering my call to ministry, God told me that I was going to have a ministry. He gave me the name of the ministry, which I wrote in my journal and shared with no one. I had no idea how this would come to pass or even the time frame of when this would happen, but nevertheless, I believed God and trusted wholeheartedly that he would lead me into my purpose and destiny.

Over the next several seasons, I spent time journeying with God. By his Spirit, he moved on me, inspiring and teaching his will and his ways. Let me also not fail to mention that where there is teaching, there is testing. As I sojourned with God, I found a deeper love in Jesus Christ that taught me to love others as I love myself, even when others did not return the same level of love to me. I learned to wholeheartedly trust him, obey him, patiently wait on him, submit to his will and ways, maintain a meek and humbled spirit, and keep my heart pure in his sight.

Nine years had passed from the time I heard God's initial call to ministry. Through the years of his teaching and testing, my gifts continued to make room for me. As God would have it in his timing, there happened to be a community located about twenty miles from my house that was looking for someone to teach weekly Bible study. Through my own personal relationship with God I have learned that what he has for me is for me. Connections were made, and one of the community residents inquired whether I was an available servant to teach. When I received their request, I prayed and asked God if this was his will and something he was calling me to do. About a week later, as I sat before the Lord in prayer, he responded and said, "I am calling you now to start the ministry." There was no questioning whether this call to start the ministry was real. God spoke the ministry's existence nine years earlier. In turn, I obeyed the Lord and started the ministry. His direct command to me was, "Go, teach the people how to live for God." The mission for the ministry was then centered around this very command given by the almighty God.

Living for God—Seven Pillars to a Virtuous Lifestyle has been inspired by the Holy Spirit to encourage, equip, and teach people around the globe to live a virtuous lifestyle for God. Amen!

Acknowledgments

To God, my Father. To Jesus Christ, my Lord and Savior, the author and finisher of my faith. To the Holy Spirit, who saw me through this journey. I give all thanks, honor, and glory to you.

To my wonderful husband, Charles, thank you for allowing me to be free in the Lord. Thank you for your unselfish love, patience, and support as I stole away into that quiet place with God.

To my two lovely daughters, Dominique and Danielle, thank you for being my breath of fresh air. Your support during the writing journey has meant so much to me. I love you dearly!

To my mother, Sandra Richmond, thank you. Words cannot express how grateful I am to have a mother like you. From birth, you have unconditionally loved and supported each of your children through their life events. Thank you for teaching us to love unconditionally like you.

To my siblings, Yvonne, Marlecia, Ryon, Jackie, Tina, and Frank, thank you for believing in the God in me as I took this writing journey.

To my dearest friend, confidant, and sister in Christ, Sharon Hargray, thank you for lending time when I needed to "touch and agree." Your prayers of intercession mean the world to me.

To Deacon Malcolm Greene, your support is priceless. I thank God daily for sending your professional and spiritual knowledge.

To Booker Richmond (aka Dad), Etta Richmond, Sonia Levi, Aubrie and Kashmere Mims, the Gardens of Stafford Bible study group, friends, and extended family, thank you for your brilliant ideas and support.

Introduction
Living Virtuously for God

The wisest man who ever lived informed us that everything we ever do or accomplish on this earth is meaningless unless we fear God and obey his commandments. In other words, unless we establish a covenant relationship with God, our lives and everything we achieved in our lives while we were living on earth means absolutely nothing.

"Everything is meaningless," says the Teacher, "completely meaningless." Keep this in mind: The Teacher was considered wise, and he taught the people everything he knew. He listened carefully to many proverbs, studying and classifying them. The Teacher sought to find just the right words to express truths clearly. The words of the wise are like cattle prods—painful but helpful. Their collected sayings are like a nail-studded stick with which a shepherd drives the sheep. But, my child, let me give you some further advice: Be careful, for writing books is endless, and much study wears you out. That's the whole story. Here now is my final conclusion: Fear God and obey his commands, for this is everyone's duty. God will judge us for everything we do, including every secret thing, whether good or bad. (Ecclesiastes 12:8–14 NLT)

Solomon, king of Israel (970 to 931 BC), heir to the throne after his father, David, was the wisest man who ever lived. In the early part of his reign, God asked Solomon specifically what he needed to fulfill his duties as king. In return, Solomon asked for wisdom to enable him to fairly judge the children of Israel. In turn, God blessed him with the wisdom and knowledge he requested. God not only blessed him with great wisdom, but because Solomon did not ask for wealth, riches, and fame, God also blessed him with those, namely great wealth, riches, and fame. In fact, he received more than any man who ever lived before him and any man who was to come after him (see 2 Chronicles 1:7–12).

Solomon's request for wisdom pleased God. I believe Solomon's wise request pleased God just as a child's wise responses and actions are pleasing to his or her parents. Growing up as children and even into adulthood, our parents are well pleased when we live according to the positive moral values they have taught us from birth. This parent-child relationship is the same with God and mankind. When mankind chooses from the heart to obey God (making him Lord of their lives) and live according to his moral household (kingdom) values and commands, God is well pleased with them and calls them his children. The Apostle John makes this point known when he says, "But as many as received him, to them gave he power to become the sons of God, even to them that believe on his name: which were born, not of blood, nor of the will of the flesh, nor of the will of man, but of God" (John 1:12–13 KJV).

Although he reigned as king, Solomon demonstrated that he needed counsel and leadership to function in his new position when he asked God to give him the wisdom to judge over the children of Israel. Instead of asking for material needs, fame, or money, Solomon asked for wisdom—God's wisdom. By asking God for wisdom, Solomon was really asking God for his partnership. Throughout Solomon's life, he was taught great moral values by his father, King David, king of Israel (1010 to 971 BC). King David trained and taught Solomon to earnestly worship and serve God with all his heart and with all his soul and to obey the commands of the Lord, his God. Before he died, David's final instructions to his son, Solomon, the new heir of his father's throne, were the following:

> Observe the requirements of the Lord your God, and follow all his ways. Keep the decrees, commands, regulations, and laws written in the Law of Moses so that you will be successful in all you do and wherever you go. If you do this, then the Lord will keep the promise he made to me. He told me, "If your descendants live as they should and follow me faithfully with all their heart and soul, one of them will always sit on the throne of Israel." (1 Kings 2:3–4 NLT)

True Wisdom Comes from God

Solomon was very young when he began his reign over Israel. Through his father's teachings, Solomon understood and recognized that God is all-knowing, all-powerful, and omnipresent, just to name a few of God's attributes, and Solomon knew this was the partnership reinforcement he was going to need in order to fulfill such a tall order of ruling over the kingdom. He recognized that being just a mere mortal, he did not know it all. He was not a great warrior/fighter with strategies for battle, and he could not be everywhere at all times to see and know the truth about all matters. But God is able. There is only one wisdom that is able to withstand the test of all matters, and that is the wisdom of God. Solomon needed God's wisdom and not the wisdom of man. The wisdom of man is full of jealously and selfish ambitions (flawed), but the wisdom of God is pure (flawless).

> If you are wise and understand God's ways, prove it by living an honorable life, doing good works with the humility that comes from wisdom. But if you are bitterly jealous and there is selfish ambition in your heart, don't cover up the truth with boasting and lying. For jealousy and selfishness are not God's kind of wisdom. Such things are earthly, unspiritual, and demonic. For wherever there is jealousy and selfish ambition, there you will find disorder and evil of every kind. But the wisdom from above is first of all pure. It is also peace loving, gentle at all times, and willing to yield to others. It is full of mercy and good deeds. It

shows no favoritism and is always sincere. And those who are peacemakers will plant seeds of peace and reap a harvest of righteousness. (James 3:13–18 NLT)

The book of Ecclesiastes is a book on wisdom written by King Solomon. The first chapter begins with Solomon's declaration that everything in life is meaningless (see Ecclesiastes 1:2). In a somewhat rhetorical way, he asks the question, "What do people get for all their hard work under the sun?" In asking that question, Solomon explores the passing of time from generation to generations, the cycles of life, the natural activity and cycles of nature, and the repetition of history. Then he summarizes that nothing is new. Everything done has been done before. With all his wisdom, he sought out to explore and understand everything under heaven. Afterward, he concluded it is all meaningless and worrisome.

After he concluded that everything is meaningless, Solomon recorded that even his great wisdom could not offer the satisfaction he was seeking. Wisdom in itself brought grief rather than satisfaction. It analyzed his problem but could not solve it. When he discovered his earthbound wisdom could not alter his fate, he became sorrowful. Without God, life is no more than repetitive cycles.[1]

There is no wisdom like the wisdom of God. We seek and search for knowledge with the hopes of obtaining more wisdom. We

---

[1]   *Notes and Bible Helps* copyright © 1988, 1989, 1990, 1991, 1993, 1996 by Tyndale House Publishers, Inc. All rights reserved. Used by Permission of Tyndale House Publishers, Inc.

go our whole lives laboring and seeking after more. We often seek the following:

- more education
- more possessions
- more money
- higher position status
- career promotions
- more love and relationships
- more excitement in life
- more pleasure
- more wisdom

Seek after God

> Fret not yourself because of evildoers;
> be not envious of wrongdoers!
> For they will soon fade like the grass
> and wither like the green herb.
> Trust in the Lord, and do good;
> dwell in the land and befriend faithfulness.
> Delight yourself in the Lord,
> and he will give you the desires of your heart.
> Commit your way to the Lord;
> trust in him, and he will act.
> He will bring forth your righteousness as the light,
> and your justice as the noonday.
> Be still before the Lord and wait patiently for him;
> fret not yourself over the one who prospers in
> his way,

over the man who carries out evil devices!
Refrain from anger, and forsake wrath!
Fret not yourself; it tends only to evil.
For the evildoers shall be cut off,
but those who wait for the Lord shall inherit the
land.
In just a little while, the wicked will be no more;
though you look carefully at his place, he will not
be there.
But the meek shall inherit the land
and delight themselves in abundant peace.
(Psalm 37:1–11 ESV)

A great amount of the population—some admit it, and some don't—want it all. Today we see many people who have started up some sort of gig, small business, or even an online video in the hopes of catching on and turning into something big. They want to gain more money, more possessions, more pleasure, higher status, etc. Well, you might be saying to yourself, "There's nothing wrong with that. We should seek to achieve more in life." And I say, "You are right. There's nothing wrong with seeking to achieve more in life. But the key here is that in many cases your seeking is self-motivated for self-gain and not God-motivated for godly gain and glory. If you are seeking prosperity for your life—and I mean every area of your life—then "delight yourself in the Lord, and he will give you the desires of your heart" (Psalm 37:4 ESV). That which you are seeking may actually be your passion and purpose, but it is not in its correct time and season. Why? Because you are relying on the wisdom of man (self and/or others), and not the wisdom of God. When we rely on the wisdom of this world, we lack the knowledge of God for our lives.

Verse 5 says, "Commit your way to the Lord; trust in him, and he will act (help you)." God is faithful to see his people through this journey called life successfully. Although the journey may entail mountains, valleys, rough terrain, stormy weather, and rivers to cross, you should put all your trust in God, and he will see you through, for it is he who has graced you with these desires, passions, and your purpose. Those who choose not to commit their way to the Lord and trust him will seek and search and elbow their way to the top only to later realize they have absolutely nothing.

Because God is all-knowing, without his knowledge and wisdom, we will never know and understand the true meaning of a fulfilled life. We will never understand the following:

- true love
- true joy
- true relationships
- true knowledge
- true wisdom
- true accomplishment
- true prosperity
- true peace and contentment

"And be not conformed to this world: but be ye transformed by the renewing of your mind, that ye may prove what is that good, and acceptable, and perfect, will of God" (Romans 12:2 KJV).

In committing our way to the Lord, we open the door to a transformed life and a renewed mind in Christ that delivers us from the wisdom of this evil world. Instead of elbowing or cheating our way to the top, we will recognize the sovereignty of God and obey his will for our lives. His will, plan, and purpose for our lives is much greater than we could ever imagine. God is faithful. He will lead you into a successful and fulfilled life that no other leader could ever offer you.

Our Sovereign Leader—There Is None Greater

Have you ever voted for a leader, whether the president, a senator, a congressman, a local official, or an organization leader, and the turnout was not in favor of the leader or official you voted for? Were you upset?

Ask yourself this question: Is that elected official really going to affect God's will and plan for my life? Sure, there may be some benefits or policies that may or may not be put into place for your gain or the gain of your family and friends, but is it really going to affect God's will for your life? The answer is *no*. God is our true sovereign leader who knows the end from the beginning. He knows what a nation and even the world needs and the timing of those needs, whether for good or for bad. Our all-knowing God also knows our needs individually, so we must set our hearts and minds to fear him and obey his commands for a blessed and prosperous life on earth. "I am the Alpha and the Omega, the Beginning and the End," says the Lord, "who is and who was and who is to come, the Almighty" (Revelation 1:8 NKJV).

Living for God: A Call to Order

In this book God is calling his people to a life of order. He is calling us to lay aside our own priorities and put his will and his work as our first priority. Many of us have grown impatient and gone ahead of God, ordering and prioritizing our lives according to our own will and not according to God's will. This level of impatience is a sign that we have lost trust in God's will and timing for our lives. Stepping out of God's will puts us on the road to disobedience, pride, and dangerously self-motivated lives. We're proclaiming God as first and foremost, but our priorities are our own. We're proclaiming our work in the name of the Lord, but the work we are putting forth is out of God's timing and order. We have left him in the dust while we run after more (whatever your *more* is).

God is our Sovereign and Most High. He is our Alpha and Omega, our beginning and our end. He knows more than we know concerning what is best for our lives. He has called and purposed us to do his work in the earth realm. However, his work must be completed according to his will and timetable. Without obeying his will, his work cannot be completed in its correct season, and many people (souls) will suffer—both the souls to be harvested as well as the souls called and entrusted to do his work.

Consider this call to order. It's a message given by God to the prophet Haggai for Judah around 520 BC after the return from exile.

> On August 29th of the second year of King
> Darius's reign, the Lord gave a message through

the prophet Haggai to Zerubbabel son of Shealtiel, governor of Judah, and to Jeshua son of Jehozadak, the high priest. "This is what the Lord of Heaven's Armies says: The people are saying, 'The time has not yet come to rebuild the house of the Lord.'" Then the Lord sent this message through the prophet Haggai: "Why are you living in luxurious houses while my house lies in ruins? This is what the Lord of Heaven's Armies says: Look at what's happening to you! You have planted much but harvest little. You eat but are not satisfied. You drink but are still thirsty. You put on clothes but cannot keep warm. Your wages disappear as though you were putting them in pockets filled with holes! "This is what the Lord of Heaven's Armies says: Look at what's happening to you! Now go up into the hills, bring down timber, and rebuild my house. Then I will take pleasure in it and be honored, says the Lord. You hoped for rich harvests, but they were poor. And when you brought your harvest home, I blew it away. Why? Because my house lies in ruins, says the Lord of Heaven's Armies, while all of you are busy building your own fine houses. It's because of you that the heavens withhold the dew and the earth produces no crops. I have called for a drought on your fields and hills—a drought to wither the grain and grapes and olive trees and all your other crops, a drought to starve you and your livestock and to ruin everything you have worked so hard to get." (Haggai 1:1–11 NLT)

In 586 BC, the Babylonian Army captured the Jews and destroyed the temple in Jerusalem. Although under Babylonian rule for seventy years, the Jews actually lived in captivity in Babylon for nearly fifty years. In 538 BC, King Cyrus issued a decree for the Jews to return back to their homeland in Jerusalem and rebuild the temple of their God. When they returned to Jerusalem, God's instruction to his prophets and leaders was to rebuild the temple. As time passed during the process of rebuilding the temple, the workers began to grow weary and become distracted. The people began to focus their attention on building their own houses and doing the work they felt necessary and not the work God commanded. Rebuilding the temple (God's work) was no longer their first priority and soon came to a halt. Absolutely no work was being done to rebuild the temple as God had instructed as their first priority.

In the Scripture text provided, the message God gave to Haggai is a call to God's people that they might bring their lives back into order and reestablish their covenant relationship with him by hearing and obeying his voice as their first priority. God sent his prophet Haggai to ask his people this question: "Why are you living in luxurious houses while my house lies in ruins" (Haggai 1:4 NLT)? This very question caused the workers and their leaders to take a long, hard look at their disorder of putting themselves first. In the message, God continues on by explaining that when the people walked in their own will and ways, he saw to it that they profited very little. The harder they worked under their own will and strength, the less they profited in their lives. God's message, delivered through his prophet Haggai, was effective, and his people repented of their ways and began rebuilding the temple through completion.

When God calls and instructs us to do a specific work he has purposed for us, we must remain focused on this calling, understand the timing, and recognize that we will require his leadership to see us through the journey. If he calls you, he has already graced you for the work. It is important that we continuously commune with God (through prayer) and hear and obey his instructions. We must remain patient and understand that God may send us through various seasons of preparation before placing us in the work he has purposed for us. God has a specific timetable to be followed, and it is important to move in his timing. When we walk in our own power and might, the results will yield only that of human strength, but when we walk in obedience to God's will and ways, the results will yield supernatural blessings and wealth.

Today God is calling his people to order. He is calling us back to the basics so that we might live virtuously and holy for him as he intended from the beginning. In this book God has given seven principles (pillars) to follow so that we can bring our lives back into a place of holiness in his sight. These seven pillars include the following:

- **Humility**—Humbling ourselves
- **Trust**—Trusting God (faith)
- **Obedience**—Obeying God
- **Love**—Loving God and others
- **Patience**—Patiently waiting on God
- **Pure Heart**—God trusting you
- **Submission**—Submit to God's will

When we choose to live for God, we conform to the moral and ethical principles of the almighty God and exalt him as the one and only Sovereign Lord. He will protect us, keep us, and guide us with his great wisdom into long life, wealth, prosperity, honor, and complete fulfillment here on earth. Amen!

SECTION 1

Intimacy

CHAPTER 1

A Covenant Relationship with God

We all are in or have been in a relationship of some type in our lives. Whether the relationship was a good experience or a bad one, the point is that it was a relationship.

A relationship can generally be defined as a connection or association we have with someone or something. A relationship can be between two people or a group of people. It can be a connection by association, by marriage, by blood, or by the Spirit. It can be an emotional, divine, corporate, or other type of tie or connection between people. Relationships can also be formed through involvement, including a sexual affair or employment. Relationships may last a lifetime or last for a season.

God Cares about Our relationships

When God created man (Adam), He recognized that the man was alone and did not have a relationship with anyone on the earth. God then caused Adam to fall into a deep sleep. While in a deep sleep, God took one of Adam's ribs and formed a woman and then brought her to him. Adam was immediately gratified by the woman God had given to him as his helper on earth. The man said, "This is now bone of my bones and flesh of my flesh; she shall be called 'woman,' for she was taken out of man" (Genesis 2:23 NIV).

God Desires a Covenant relationship with Us

Many people may have pondered the question, "Which came first, humanity's need for a relationship with God or God's desire for a relationship with humanity?" Here is the answer: "We love Him, because He first loved us," explains the apostle John (1 John 4:19 KJV). John also tells us, "In this is love, not that we loved God but that he loved us and sent his Son to be the atoning sacrifice for our sins" (1 John 4:10 NRSV). Clearly it was God's desire and plan to establish a relationship between human beings and himself.

We must keep in mind God's purpose for creating us. God designed human beings to reflect His very character—to be like Him. "In the day when God created man, He made him in the likeness of God" (Genesis 5:1 NASB). "God created man in His own image, in the image of God He created him; male and female He created them" (Genesis 1:27 NASB).

God instituted a covenant relationship with ancient Israel when He said, "I will walk among you and be your God, and you will be My people" (Leviticus 26:12 NIV). These few words summarize what God wants in his relationship with people. Notice the two aspects of God's simple statement. First he expresses his desire that we acknowledge and accept him as the Supreme Being. Then he expresses his desire to associate with—to have a relationship with—those who accept him as their God.

Once we understand that God desires a relationship with us, we should more than ever recognize that we truly need him. The apostle Paul reminds us, "There is no question of our having sufficient power in ourselves: we cannot claim anything as our own. The power we have comes from God" (2 Corinthians 3:5 REB).[2]

> This command I am giving you today is not too difficult for you to understand, and it is not beyond your reach. It is not kept in heaven, so distant that you must ask, "Who will go up to heaven and bring it down so we can hear it and obey?" It is not kept beyond the sea, so far away that you must ask, "Who will cross the sea to bring it to us so we can hear it and obey?" No, the message is very close at hand; it is on your lips and in your heart so that you can obey it. Now listen! Today I am giving you a choice between life and death, between prosperity and disaster. For I command you this day to love the Lord your God and to keep his commands, decrees, and regulations by walking in his ways. If you do this, you will live and multiply, and the Lord

---

[2]   *God Wants a Relationship with Us.* Used with permission. "Bible Study Course Lesson 7," published by United Church of God, an international association. © 2015 United Church of God. www.ucg.org/bible-study-course.

your God will bless you and the land you are about to enter and occupy. But if your heart turns away and you refuse to listen, and if you are drawn away to serve and worship other gods, then I warn you now that you will certainly be destroyed. You will not live a long, good life in the land you are crossing the Jordan to occupy. Today I have given you the choice between life and death, between blessings and curses. Now I call on heaven and earth to witness the choice you make. Oh, that you would choose life, so that you and your descendants might live! You can make this choice by loving the Lord your God, obeying him, and committing yourself firmly to him. He is the key to your life. And if you love and obey the Lord, you will live long in the land the Lord swore to give your ancestors Abraham, Isaac, and Jacob. (Deuteronomy 30:11–20 NLT)

Who Is God that We Should Choose Him?

In the previous passage and throughout the book of Deuteronomy, God makes it known what it will profit us to engage in a covenant relationship with him. It is God's desire that all of humankind have a relationship with Him, but he does not force us to have a relationship with him. He gives us a choice just as the previous Scripture explains, and that choice is a life or death situation. Verse 15 says, "Now Listen! Today I am giving you a choice between life and death, between prosperity and disaster."

The apostle John says, "In the beginning was the Word, and the Word was with God, and the Word was God. The same was in the beginning with God. All things were made by him; and without him was not any thing made that was made. In him was life; and the life was the light of men. And the light shineth in darkness; and the darkness comprehended it not" (John 1:1–4 KJV).

The Word (Jesus Christ) was present in the beginning with God, even from creation. Because Jesus Christ is God, He is alive eternally. Life comes from God through Christ. When we choose Jesus Christ, by grace we are given the free gift of eternal life. In Christ there is life, and that life is the light of humanity. So I dare you to choose life and let your light so shine before humanity that people see your good works (your obedience to God, your faithfulness to God, your submission to God, etc.) and glorify God the Father, who is in heaven (see Matthew 5:16).

Deuteronomy 30:16 (NLT) says, "For I command you this day to love the Lord your God and to keep his commands, decrees, and regulations by walking in his ways. If you do this, you will live and multiply, and the Lord your God will bless you and the land you are about to enter and occupy." By choosing life (accepting Jesus Christ and obeying his will), God promises an eternal and blessed life. By choosing death (rejecting Christ and disobeying him), you are sure to live a cursed and unfulfilled life.

My Own Covenant relationship with God

From birth, my mother took me to church. As a child, along with my siblings, we were loaded in the car every Sunday to attend early morning Sunday school classes. Afterward, we had to sit through a boring hour of church service. As young teens, my sister and I were invited to sing in the church choir. I found singing in the choir allowed me to understand more about God. Singing the lyrics of the songs enabled me to learn more about who he is overall as well as who he is to me personally. At the age of thirteen, I was baptized in water. Although I understood the baptism to be a very special covenant I was making with God, no one was really teaching me about having an intimate relationship with God. In fact, I don't believe too many adults were seeking a personal and intimate relationship with God. I remember how week after week the preacher preached, and there were some amens and some emotional shouts; however, I did not really witness or experience lives changing. Most families left the church service in the same condition they had come.

I guess one might say that I grew up going to church but had no clue that true worship involved an intimate relationship with God. Frankly I don't believe many of the adults there understood what a true relationship with God meant. Most of us lived in the same small town and community, so it was inevitable that we would witness one another's lifestyles outside the four walls of the church. But despite a lack of godly wisdom and understanding, enough seeds (God's Word) were planted within my heart that when I got old, I did not depart from it. King Solomon says in Proverbs 22:6 (KJV), "Train up a child in the way he should go: and when he is old, he will not depart from it."

As I came into adulthood, married at the age of twenty-four, and began to have a family and children of my own, I began to seek and want more from God. First and foremost I wanted to raise my children in church just as I was raised. The seed had been planted from my childhood. I believed in my heart the words of Proverbs 22:6, which says, "Train up a child in the way he should go." So regardless of what I lacked in covenant relationship teachings, the seeds planted fell on good ground. Enough of these Scripture seeds, planted and germinating from my youth, led to an increase in my faith and my heart wanting more from God.

I joined a local church that I had been attending not long after I moved to the Washington, DC, area. I continued in the same traditional and religious mind-set that attending church service was the only way to worship and fellowship with God, and I also felt that my attendance checked the box for what God requires from us. After my daughters were born and as soon as they reached the appropriate age, I put them in Sunday school. I found ways for us to get involved more in the church through participation in special church programs, especially during various religious holidays.

Our church had a liturgical dance ministry for both adults and children. One day in church service while the dance ministry ministered, my oldest daughter leaned over and asked if she could be in the dance ministry. I replied to her and said we would check into it. Not long afterward, I spoke with the dance ministry director and expressed to her my daughter's interest in joining the dance ministry. She spoke with excitement and said, "Yes, please come to our rehearsal next Sunday afternoon." After they attended the rehearsal, both girls were motivated and wanted to be a part of the liturgical dance ministry. Later the dance ministry drew me in as well, and within a couple of months, I joined the ministry.

Joining the liturgical dance ministry was a turning point in my life, and it was a vehicle that drove me right into the presence of the almighty God. Through liturgical dance training and teachings, I learned that it's not a performance but that my dance must point people to God. Through dance, I began to learn about living and being holy before the Lord. In other words, I must live what I dance. My life must reflect that about which I am dancing. Through dance, I communed with God, and the more I communed with God, the more I wanted a deeper and more intimate relationship with Him. I came to realize that through this relationship with God, every void that I ever had was being filled. As I began to fall further in love with God, I began to ask him for a deeper and more intimate relationship.

Although I had found the true and living God through liturgical dance ministry, I still had impure activities in my life that prevented me from reaching a pure and intimate relationship with God. I needed to shed the impure for the pure. I needed complete healing in my soul. Despite my issue, I continue my search for a deeper relationship with God.

Then one day I faced a life crisis. I was moving in the wrong direction, and I was living according to my own will and desires. My husband and I were about to get a divorce. I got into a car accident, and my life was falling apart right before my eyes. But when I humbled myself and prayed, I cried out to God with a heart of repentance, and he heard me.

A few days later, while I was working in my office, God spoke into my spirit and said, "Don't leave your husband."

I thought, *What?*

He said it again, "Don't leave your husband. Your home is where you belong."

I took a deep sigh, and I thought to myself, *I know I'm not hearing this.* I had already purchased a new townhouse and was preparing to move within the next couple of weeks. At the same time, I considered the matter and knew that I did not want to disobey God. I did not know what to do, so I decided for the moment that maybe I was imagining that God had spoken this to me. I kept this to myself and did not share it with anyone.

The next day while I was at work, I spoke on the phone with a dear friend who worked in the same building. She asked me if I wanted to have lunch with her that day. She is a born-again believer, and I know when we get together, we are going to praise and worship God. So we agreed on a time, and I met her in her office before we went to sit in the cafeteria. At that time she was working a reception desk and was unable to leave until someone relieved her. While we were waiting for her stand-in to come, we chatted, and in the midst of our chat, she looked at me with sorrow in her eyes and said, "Are you really going to leave your husband?" At that moment my heart sank, and before I could think of something to say, her desk phone rang. I thought, *Yes, saved by the bell.* I was still nervous about her asking, and I didn't know how I was going to respond. When she completed the call and hung up, I was on pins and needles. We ended up getting on another topic, and boy did I feel relieved. Once we reached the cafeteria and sat down to eat, we began to talk about our lives and glorifying God in our lives. Then my friend looked at me again with sorrowful eyes and asked, "Armenta, are you really going to leave your husband?"

I intently stared back at her, and when I did, giant tears began to flow down my face. I responded, "No, God came to me yesterday and told me not to leave my husband." I went on to tell her that I would never want to disobey God, so I was not going to get a divorce.

She, too, began to weep and explained, "God told me to tell you not to get a divorce, but I did not know how to tell you. So I asked the Holy Spirit to help me find a way to tell you." We both rejoiced during our entire lunch break, and when we departed to go back to our offices, I told her that I would return home that evening and talk with my husband about the matter in hopes of his heart being humbled enough that we could agree.

What I did not know was that my husband had been praying to God, asking him to save his marriage. That evening my husband and I talked, and he could not believe what I was saying. He said that he had already prepared himself mentally and emotionally for me and the girls to move out and the coming divorce. I explained to him that it was God's will for us to stay married, and I did not want to go against God's will. I asked him to think about it overnight and pray and ask God for himself.

The next day when my husband returned home from work, I was standing in the kitchen, preparing dinner. When he walked in, he came over to me, kissed me on the cheek, and said, "Everything is going to be all right."

God saved and restored our marriage, saved our souls, healed our hearts, and made our family whole. Not only did he freely gift us with salvation, but he also blessed us with a pure covenant relationship with him. After I experienced the power of God in my life, I completely surrendered my will to his will for my life. I knew without a shadow of a doubt. "I have been crucified with Christ and I no longer live, but Christ lives in me. The life I live in the body, I live by faith in the Son of God, who loved me and gave himself for me" (Galatians 2:20 NIV).

Not long after that, I answered His call for me to go into ministry. I was honored to be called by God and accepted the assignment. In my prayers I sought to live and walk in extreme obedience to God's commands and instructions concerning my life. For over twenty years, my covenant relationship with God has been one of humility, love, obedience, trust, patience, submission, and a pure heart (God trusting me). Every second of every minute, every minute of every hour, and every hour of every day, my life is a journey with the almighty God, for it is he who forgave me and saved me.

A Model Leader's relationship with God

After the death of Moses the servant of the Lord, the Lord said to Joshua the son of Nun, Moses' assistant, "Moses my servant is dead. Now therefore arise, go over this Jordan, you and all this people, into the land that I am giving to them, to the people of Israel. Every place that the sole of your foot will tread upon I have given to you, just as I promised to Moses. From the wilderness and this Lebanon as far as the great river, the river Euphrates, all the land of the Hittites to the Great Sea toward the going down of the sun shall be your territory. No man shall be able to stand before you all the days of your life. Just as I was with Moses, so I will be with you. I will not leave you or forsake you. Be strong and courageous, for you shall cause this people to inherit the land that I swore to their fathers to give them. Only be strong and very courageous, being careful to do according to all the law that Moses my servant commanded you. Do not turn from it to the right hand or to the left, that you may have good success wherever you go. This Book of the Law shall not depart from your mouth, but you shall meditate on it day and night, so that you may be careful to do according to all that is written in it. For then you will make your way prosperous, and then you will have good success. Have I not commanded you? Be strong and courageous. Do not be frightened, and do not be dismayed, for

the Lord your God is with you wherever you go."
(Joshua 1:1–9 ESV)

Joshua, an assistant to Moses, was chosen by God to lead the children of Israel into their Promised Land (Canaan). God promised Joshua just as he promised Moses, namely that God had given to him every place that the soles of his feet would tread.

Joshua trusted God and chose to keep a covenant relationship with him. He exemplified an upright and covenant lifestyle before all of Israel. He was a profound leader of the nation because of his godly life of obedience and service unto God. Joshua was a man who was not ashamed to "let his light so shine before men that they see his good works, and glorify God" (Matthew 5:16).

God had a hand in all the battles fought in order for Joshua and Israel to victoriously take and possess their Promised Land. Imagine our leaders today following after and maintaining a covenant relationship with the all-powerful, all-knowing, and omnipresent God. Unity, liberty, and justice for all would flow throughout the land.

As a model leader, Joshua kept his vows to the Most High. He maintained covenant with God and did not turn to the left or to the right. When we, too, follow in the footsteps of Joshua by maintaining a covenant relationship with God, our lives become victorious and fulfilling in every way, even in the midst of our storms and struggles.

Joshua would not have been the great leader he was without his covenant relationship with the almighty God. As Israel's leader, Joshua found it necessary when he was addressing the nation to ask whom they chose.

> Now fear the Lord and serve him with all faithfulness. Throw away the gods your forefathers worshiped beyond the River and in Egypt, and serve the Lord. But if serving the Lord seems undesirable to you, then choose for yourselves this day whom you will serve, whether the gods your forefathers served beyond the River, or the gods of the Amorites, in whose land you are living. But as for me and my household, we will serve the Lord. (Joshua 24:14–15 NIV)

In verse 14, Joshua encourages the people to fear the Lord and serve him wholeheartedly. He says, "If you refuse to serve the Lord, then choose today who you will serve." In other words, Joshua is asking them to make a decision from their hearts. It is one thing to say you will worship the Lord, but it is quite another to live a life dedicated to the Lord. We cannot half heartedly serve the Lord. Our commitment in the relationship either involves our whole self or none—no fence-straddling allowed. Joshua then makes it clear to the entire nation, "As for me and my household (family), we will serve the Lord."

Whom Do You Choose to Serve and Obey?

This is the most important decision you will ever have to make in your life. By not making a decision, nonetheless, the decision is made by your actions, specifically the how and who you are living for. Your decision must come from your heart and soul, and since it is the most important decision in your life, it should not be made haphazardly. Take time to weigh your options. Deuteronomy 30:15 (NLT) says, "Now Listen! Today I am giving you a choice between life and death, between prosperity and disaster."

We cannot live and lead with victorious purpose until we choose to come into a covenant relationship with God through Jesus Christ. When you are in covenant with God, he will see to it that you have uncommon favor, dominion, and the authority to do the miraculous just like Joshua. Joshua's leadership had such an effect that the nation kept its covenant relationship with God for many years succeeding his death. Joshua's legacy was one of honor and respect by all, ranging from his high-ranking officials to the everyday layperson.

CHAPTER 2

Communion with God

What is a relationship without some form of communication? In chapter 1, we generally defined a relationship as a connection or association we have with someone or something. So how might our relationships begin? We obtain and maintain relationships with others through communication.

Our God is a living God who desires an intimate and more personal involvement, connection, and association with us. Communion is a key ingredient for an intimate relationship with God. Communion is more than just common communication. It is a close and intimate partnership. How will our communion with God aid in the growth of our relationship with him and result in an experience like none other? First John 4:19 (KJV) says, "We love him, because he first loved us." Our relationship began with God well before we recognized or even knew we could have a relationship with him. God's creation of mankind is an expression of His love.

> So God created man in his own image, in the
> image of God created he him; male and female

created he them. And God blessed them, and God said unto them, Be fruitful, and multiply, and replenish the earth, and subdue it: and have dominion over the fish of the sea, and over the fowl of the air, and over every living thing that moveth upon the earth. (Genesis 1:27–28 KJV)

When he made mankind, he made them in the likeness of his own image. Not only did he create mankind in his own image, but he then blessed them and spoke blessings over their lives too, giving them dominion over the animals and over everything living on earth. Creating us in his image and giving us dominion are all reflections of him. He created mankind to possess commonality with himself; thereby enabling us to understand or comprehend him better. When he created humanity, God began communicating with us.

Our relationship with God grows when we spend time getting to know him. God, on the other hand, already knows us (see Jeremiah 1:5) and desires daily communion with us. Our intimate partnership with God is an act of sharing and maintaining close fellowship. The more time we spend in communion with God through his Word, through prayer and meditation, through praising him, and worshipping him, the more we will get to know him and grow closer to him.

If you have chosen to fear God and obey his commandments, then you have chosen a covenant relationship with him. In order to keep in covenant with him, you must display a constant and conscious effort of humility, trust (faithfulness), obedience, submission, patience, pure-hearted, and love. These seven pillars uphold one another and are the ingredients to a healthy and holy lifestyle in the eyes of God.

Throughout the Bible, God communicated boundaries in his covenant relationship with us. For starters, he expects us to be holy as he, the Lord our God, is holy. "And ye shall be holy unto me: for I the Lord am holy, and have severed you from other people, that ye should be mine" (Leviticus 20:26 KJV).

A covenant relationship with God (a life of holiness) means we must live in obedience according to his standards and will. He is our Lord, and he sets us apart from those who have not chosen him. Those who have not chosen him are disobedient and destined for death and curses (see Deuteronomy 30:15–20).

Peter explained it best when he said,

> So roll up your sleeves, put your mind in gear, be totally ready to receive the gift that's coming when Jesus arrives. Don't lazily slip back into those old grooves of evil, doing just what you feel like doing. You didn't know any better then; you do now. As obedient children, let yourselves be pulled into a way of life shaped by God's life, a life energetic and blazing with holiness. God said, "I am holy; you be holy." You call out to God for help and he helps—he's a good Father that way. But don't forget, he's also a responsible Father, and won't let you get by with sloppy living. Your life is a journey you must travel with a deep consciousness of God. It cost God plenty to get you out of that dead-end, empty-headed

life you grew up in. He paid with Christ's sacred blood, you know. He died like an unblemished, sacrificial lamb. And this was no afterthought. Even though it has only lately—at the end of the ages—become public knowledge, God always knew he was going to do this for you. It's because of this sacrificed Messiah, whom God then raised from the dead and glorified, that you trust God, that you know you have a future in God. Now that you've cleaned up your lives by following the truth, love one another as if your lives depended on it. Your new life is not like your old life. Your old birth came from mortal sperm; your new birth comes from God's living Word. Just think: a life conceived by God himself! That's why the prophet said,

> The old life is a grass life,
> its beauty as short-lived as wildflowers;
> Grass dries up, flowers droop,
> God's Word goes on and on forever.

This is the Word that conceived the new life in you. (1 Peter 1:13–25 MSG)

Holiness is not about your outward appearances—how you dress, your deeds, the church you attend, how much education you have achieved, or other rules set by man. It is about your inward character traits of obedience, trust, submission, humility, among others, traits that are holy and acceptable to God. Do you fear him with a childlike fear that causes you to obey him?

Are you willing to be like Christ and submit to the will of God for every area of your life?

Communion with God—A Place of rest

Jesus said in Matthew 11:28–30 (ESV), "Come to me, all who labor and are heavy laden, and I will give you rest. Take my yoke upon you, and learn from me, for I am gentle and lowly in heart, and you will find rest for your souls. For my yoke is easy, and my burden is light."

In Christ we can find rest for our soul. The term *rest* in this occurrence means repose.

Repose can be defined as a place where someone can find rest and/or peacefulness. Are you tired? Have you been handling life in your own strength and might? In your communion with God, you will find it to be a place where your mind, heart, and soul can rest peacefully and calmly even in the midst of daily trials. Communion with God becomes a matter of your heart seeking his will and not your own will. Your heart seeks to be led by his Spirit in all that you do. When you seek him daily through prayer and/or through his Word concerning all matters, he will instruct you. If you choose to listen and obey his instructions, burdens and weariness are lifted. He promises and assures us that he will take care of us even in the most challenging times of life.

Repose can also be defined as putting your complete trust in something or someone. Not only is Christ offering us rest through peace in our heart, mind, and soul, but he is also saying,

"Put your complete confidence and trust in me. Come to me with all your matters, even the most difficult or embarrassing matters. I am meek and humble, and I will not judge you. I only want to make your life one of good quality." It's comforting to know we have someone (a confidant) we can go to and share all of our secrets, hurts, pains, and any other issues on our minds without it leaking out to others or being displayed on the Internet. Human confidants are wonderful, but the greatest confidant is God himself. Human confidants could possibly let you down, but with God, confidentiality is sacred. Human confidants mainly listen and maybe give some advice, but with God, He is all-knowing, all-powerful, omnipresent, etc. He has the exact answers you need. He will provide the solutions. His hand is extended. The invitation is there. All you must do is come into covenant with him and commune with him daily.

Communion with God through His Word

God makes himself available for us so that we can know him through Christ (his Word). To know the Word (Jesus Christ) is to know God. "In the beginning was the Word, and the Word was with God, and the Word was God" (John 1:1 KJV).

The more we study the Word of God, the more we will know Christ. Christ (the Word) was in the beginning with God, and he is God. The gospels (Matthew, Mark, Luke, and John) tell us the story of Jesus Christ's life on the earth—his birth, his life, his ministry, his death, his burial, his resurrection, and his ascension. Through studying the gospels we are able to obtain knowledge, get understanding, and witness the manifestation of Jesus Christ throughout the Bible. There is no greater way to get to know Christ intimately than through his Word. Jesus said, "My Father has entrusted everything to me. No one truly knows the Son except the Father, and no one truly knows the Father except the Son and those to whom the Son chooses to reveal him" (Matthew 11:27 NLT).

"In the Old Testament, *know* means more than knowledge. It implies intimate relationship. The communion between God the Father and God the Son is the core of their relationship. For anyone else to know God, God must reveal himself to that person, by the Son's choice. How fortunate we are that Jesus has clearly revealed God to us, as well as his truth and how much we can know him."[3]

Just as the communion between God the Father and God the Son is the core of their relationship, so is our communion with God through his Word the core of our relationship with him. We must allow his Spirit to lead us in our reading and studying the Word of God. Through his leadership and guidance, we will find the answers to life questions and solutions to personal problems as well as communal or world problems. Remember from the introduction of this book that King Solomon explained that history merely repeats itself. It has all been done before. Nothing under the sun is truly new (see Ecclesiastes 1:9). The answers to our questions and the solutions to all problems can be found in our communion with God through his Word.

---

[3]   *Notes and Bible Helps* copyright © 1988, 1989, 1990, 1991, 1993, 1996 by Tyndale House Publishers, Inc. All rights reserved. Used by Permission of Tyndale House Publishers, Inc.

Frequent study and meditation of his Word increases our communication with God. God speaks to us through his Word—whether he is giving answers to our prayers or comforting words during a storm or life crisis. We must learn to depend on God to see us through the good, the bad, and the ugly.

Communion with God through Prayer and Meditation

In any healthy relationship, communication must be two-way. There's a speaker, and there is a listener. Although God is our Supreme, Most High, and Most Sovereign God, he is not interested in dominating the conversations in his intimate fellowship with us. God expects, and most of all desires us to talk to him. We can bring anything before him in confidence and know that the conversation will not go any further than the two of us. Here are some questions to ponder:

> How can God answer our questions if we don't
> ask him?
> How can God solve our problems if we don't
> tell him?
> How can God open the door if we don't knock?
> How can God find us if we don't seek him?
> How can God give to us if we don't explain our
> need to him?
> How can God hear us if we don't call his name?
> How can we know God's will concerning a matter
> if we don't approach him in prayer?

Perhaps these questions will help us to understand that we must engage in conversation with God in order for change to happen. A balance between prayer and meditation—a time to keep silence, and a time to speak (see Ecclesiastes 3:7) —is the key. Prayer and meditation is our lifeline to both talk to God and to hear from God. How can we obey God if we don't hear and receive his instructions and guidance? Spend quality time with God daily, communing with him in his presence, not just one time a day but multiple times in a day.

If you don't already have one, I encourage you to pick out a quiet spot in your house and consider it your place that you meet with God. If you don't have an extra room to call your prayer room, you can use a spot on the couch or a corner of a room. (You can put a towel or blanket down.). Believe it or not, I have friends who steal away to the bathroom and spend time with God. This works even if you have a house full of people or kids. They have to go to sleep at some time or another. My favorite quiet time with God is during the wee hours. It's the perfect atmosphere for his still, small voice to speak into my spirit. You can speak to God and tell him, "This is our spot!" Then anoint the place with oil and sanctify it.

Please understand that communing with God through prayer is not just something that occurs at home. We can pray and meditate while we are driving, riding, walking, waiting at the doctor's office, waiting to eat meals (even when eating out), and we can pray with and for others in a public place.

When I travel, I usually sanctify a spot in my hotel room where I want to meet with God. I try not to pray in bed. That is a recipe for dropping back off to sleep. So I usually seek out a spot in the room, whether sitting at the desk or in the side chair, or if I want to lay prostrate, I will put a couple of towels down on the floor. The important thing is that your heart seek communion with God no matter where you are. "And I tell you, ask, and it will be given to you; seek, and you will find; knock, and it will be opened to you. For everyone who asks receives, and the one who seeks finds, and to the one who knocks it will be opened" (Luke 11:9–10 ESV). "For I know the plans I have for you, declares the Lord, plans for welfare and not for evil, to give you a future and a hope. Then you will call upon me and come and pray to me, and I will hear you. You will seek me and find me, when you seek me with all your heart" (Jeremiah 29:11–13 ESV).

Communion with God through Praise and Worship

Only God is worthy of our praise and worship.

Praise

> Praise the Lord!
> Praise God in his sanctuary; praise him in his
> mighty heavens! Praise him for his mighty deeds;
> praise him according to his excellent greatness!
> Praise him with trumpet sound;
> praise him with lute and harp!
> Praise him with tambourine and dance;
> praise him with strings and pipe! Praise him with
> sounding cymbals; praise him with loud clashing
> cymbals!
> Let everything that has breath praise the Lord!
> Praise the Lord!
> (Psalm 150:1–6 ESV)

When praises go up (to God), blessings come down (from God). What is praise that our Lord delights in it so much that he responds with blessings from heaven? What is praise that the previous Scripture declares that everything that has breath (life) must praise the Lord?

Praise is a form of communication. Praise is a positive expression about or to someone or something. In our case, we are discussing communion with God, so our praise to God is an expression of our gratitude, our love, and our respect for all he has done for us, all he is doing, and all he is going to do in our lives. Praise can also be a weapon of our warfare. We can praise God in advance for the victory over our circumstances. Our praise to God can shake up the Enemy's camp, cause confusion in the Enemy's camp, tear down Enemy walls, and change the atmosphere.

We could write an entire book on praise, but for the sake of this chapter, I will attempt to include the nuggets we need to understand the importance and the awesomeness of communing with God through praise. There are many ways to praise God—through spoken words, through song, through dance (movement), through musical instruments, etc. In addition to the many ways to praise God, there are several forms of praise.

The word *praise* is mentioned 248 times in the Bible. Not every occurrence of the word carries the same meaning or speaks of the same form of praise. Let us explore a few.

Genesis 29:35 (ESV) says, "And she conceived again and bore a son, and said, 'This time I will praise the Lord.' Therefore she called his name Judah. Then she ceased bearing." The word praise in this passage is the Hebrew word *yadah*, which means "to hold out the hand" (i.e., to extend the hands), mainly to express admiration or worship. We can praise God through the use of our hands by extending as well as clapping.

First Chronicle 29:13 (ESV) says, "And now we thank you, our God, and praise your glorious name." The word praise in this passage is the Hebrew word *halal*, which means "to boast about the Lord; to be clamorously foolish; to rave; or to celebrate his greatness." This form of praise tells us that we can praise God with great excitement and boast in the Lord, causing us to shine even brighter in his eyes. This kind of praise atmosphere causes his glory to manifest mightily.

Psalm 63:3 (ESV) says, "Because your steadfast love is better than life, my lips will praise you." The word praise in this passage is the Hebrew word *shabach*, which means "to speak loudly." We can give God a shout of praise. (*Hallelujah!*)

Psalm 119:171 (ESV) says, "My lips will pour forth praise, for you teach me your statutes." The word praise in this passage is the Hebrew word *tehillah*, which refers to a hymn or song of praise. We can praise God in our song to him.

After we explore the forms of praise listed previously, we can now understand that our praise is an awesome way of communing with God. God is responsive to our praise. Psalm 22:3 says that he inhabits the praises of his people. He responds to our praise by inviting us into his presence for a pure worship experience.

Worship

Where praise is a full- on outward expression to God, worship is a more personal and inward expression from the heart. Praise prepares the heart for the worship experience. Worship is placing yourself in a lowly and submissive place mentally, psychologically, spiritually, and even physically. It is where God overshadows you with his presence.

Worship is an action. It is our overwhelming expression of honor and respect to our great God.

Just as with praise, worship is a form of communication. Communion with God through worship lands us in the secret place of the Most High. This secret place is where God shares His great wisdom, the mysteries of his kingdom, his plans and purposes for you, and much more according to his divine will. As I said previously in the section on praise, God responds to our praise by inviting us into his presence for the worship experience. Worship is extremely intimate communion with God where we humble ourselves and acknowledge that he is supreme with glory, majesty, splendor, and power.

Although the presence of God is everywhere, we cannot enter into his presence in any kind of way or on our own terms. There is a pattern for coming into the presence of God. First our hearts and minds must be prepared through offering up sacrificial praises to God. This is another reason why praise is important.

> "Through Jesus, therefore, let us continually offer
> to God a sacrifice of praise—the fruit of lips that
> confess his name. And do not forget to do good

and to share with others, for with such sacrifices God is pleased" (Hebrews 13:15–16 NIV).

A sacrificial praise that is pleasing to God enables him to transform our hearts into feeling a softer state of love, compassion, and adoration toward him, which brings us into the worship experience, an intimate time of communion exchanges between God and us. God conveys to us how much we are loved by him, and we in turn poor out to God, telling him how much we love and adore him.

Praise and worship are different phases of communication with God, but they go hand in hand. You cannot have one without the other. True worship cannot be experienced without first offering up a sacrifice of praise. Likewise, you cannot offer up a sacrificial praise without the manifestation of the worship following behind.

I had a friend who once told me that she was a worshipper and that she was not much into praising. When she told me this, I did not pay much attention to what she was saying, because we were actually sitting in a church service and my mind and heart were focused on God. But some days later, I began thinking about what she had said, and I thought, *Wow, if you are not into praising, then you definitely are not into worshipping either.* Communion with God through praise brings us into the worship experience with God.

The Pillars

CHAPTER 3

Trust

Relationships must be built on some sort of trust (faith). Trust is built on the integrity of one's character. The more we personally learn of the reliability and integrity of one's character, the more we grow in our faith or trust in that person. Are they who they say they are? Are they men or women of their word?

At the introduction of our new connections or associations, we will need to exercise some level of faith. We might think to ourselves, *I don't know this person, but there seems to be some commonality between us, so let's see what happens.* For most of us, because trust has not been built, we may have some concern in the beginning and keep our guards up. As stranger among stranger, we only disclose personal information on an as-needed basis. Perhaps if the new connection or association begins with an introduction from a trusted friend who acknowledges the trustworthiness of the one he or she is connecting us with, we are more inclined to open up to the new connection. But in any case, trust plays a major role in whether the relationship will grow or not.

Trusting God (Our Faith)

Our trust in God is directly related to our level of faith in him. How much faith do you have in God to trust him in a relationship? Coming into a relationship with God will require trust from both you and God. For this chapter on trust, we are going to focus on trusting God. In a later chapter, we will then focus on God trusting us.

> At that time the disciples came to Jesus and asked, "Who is the greatest in the kingdom of heaven?" He called a little child and had him stand among them. And he said: "I tell you the truth, unless you change and become like little children, you will never enter the kingdom of heaven. Therefore, whoever humbles himself like this child is the greatest in the kingdom of heaven. And whoever welcomes a little child like this in my name welcomes me." "But if anyone causes one of these little ones who believe in me to sin, it would be better for him to have a large millstone hung around his neck and to be drowned in the depths of the sea. (Matthew 18:1–6 NIV)

The previous Scripture passage is a perfect depiction of how trust begins in our lives. From the time we are born, we must trust that someone will care for us. As children unable to care for ourselves, we learn to trust our parents or guardians for the provision of food, clothing, and protection. Being unable to care for one's self is a humbling place (lowly position). It is humbling because for whatever the reason or circumstance, the person is unable to care for his or herself. The situation puts the individual in a place of dependence and/or reliance upon someone else to do the things required for his or her survival. Adults may think they deserve to be cared for and waited on, but with children, their position of humility is more evident. Chances are they have not learned that prideful behavior. It's pride that says, "I deserve it."

Children are vulnerable and subject to whatever evil cards this world might deal to them. So a child must keep a spirit of hope that someone (parents/guardians, etc.) will raise them and protect them until they are able to protect and care for themselves. Jesus is looking for us to humble ourselves and to learn to trust him just as a child is humble and trusts his parents (with childlike faith). Without childlike faith in God through Jesus Christ, it is impossible to enter the kingdom of heaven. Just as a child is vulnerable in the trust of their parents, so are God's children vulnerable in their trust (faith walk) with God. In trusting God, they should also trust in the family of God. In verse 6, Jesus warns against anyone who causes a child of God to stumble. The consequences are severe.

In Proverbs 3, King Solomon shares the wisdom given to him by his father, King David, concerning the topic of trusting God.

> My child, never forget the things I have taught you. Store my commands in your heart. If you do this, you will live many years, and your life will be satisfying. Never let loyalty and kindness leave you! Tie them around your neck as a reminder. Write them deep within your heart. Then you

will find favor with both God and people, and you will earn a good reputation. Trust in the Lord with all your heart; do not depend on your own understanding. Seek his will in all you do, and he will show you which path to take. (Proverbs 3:1–6 NLT)

Trust is something learned and developed over time. It takes time to determine if a man is who he says he is. David was confidently able to present Solomon with the wisdom in verse 5 because David knew God for himself. King David was an obedient servant of the Lord and worshipped God wholeheartedly. David was a warrior and depended wholeheartedly on God for direction and help, causing him to be victorious in all his battles. David sought the Lord concerning all matters in his life. Although David's household had its share of dysfunction, David continued to trust in the Lord with all his heart. Solomon grew up watching and listening to his father and learned to trust God from the example set by his father. In order for Solomon to exercise that wisdom, he had to get to know and trust God for himself. When the opportunity came in Solomon's life for him to trust God, he did just that. During his reign as king, Solomon sought the Lord for his wisdom concerning Israel. When God realized the desire of Solomon's heart was to serve him, he blessed Solomon's life with great wisdom, wealth, riches, and honor.

Do you truly know God for yourself ? What do you know about God? Is he who he says he is? In chapter 2, we discussed communion with God through his Word. The best way to get to know God for yourself is through the Word of God.

Through the Word of God, we get to know the true integrity of God's character. We see God's faithfulness throughout the Bible. He made promises to the world, nations, and individuals, and he was faithful to and kept all of his promises. Faithfulness is one of the many character traits of God.

Those who are faithful are true to their word and keep promises. They put great care in the work they perform. A faithful person is reliable and trustworthy in any situation or circumstance. I believe it's safe to conclude that *faithfulness* is a character trait of integrity. We can put our trust in God because of his proven faithfulness toward us as well as others.

God's Promise to Abraham

The Lord had said to Abram, "Leave your native country, your relatives, and your father's family, and go to the land that I will show you. I will make you into a great nation. I will bless you and make you famous, and you will be a blessing to others. I will bless those who bless you and curse those who treat you with contempt. All the families on earth will be blessed through you." So Abram departed as the Lord had instructed, and Lot went with him. Abram was seventy-five years old when he left Haran. He took his wife, Sarai, his nephew Lot, and all his wealth—his livestock and all the people he had taken into his household at Haran—and headed for the land of Canaan. When they arrived in Canaan, Abram traveled through the land as far as Shechem. There he set up camp beside the oak of Moreh. At that time, the area was inhabited by Canaanites. Then the Lord appeared to Abram and said, "I will give this land to your descendants." And Abram built an altar there and dedicated it to the Lord, who had appeared to him. After that, Abram traveled south and set up camp in the hill country, with Bethel to the west and Ai to the east. There he built another altar and dedicated it to the Lord, and he worshiped the Lord. Then Abram continued traveling south by stages toward the Negev. (Genesis 12:1–9 NLT)

Some time later, the Lord spoke to Abram in a vision and said to him, "Do not be afraid, Abram, for I will protect you, and your reward will be great." But Abram replied, "O Sovereign Lord, what good are all your blessings when I don't even have a son? Since you've given me no children, Eliezer of Damascus, a servant in my household, will inherit all my wealth. You have given me no descendants of my own, so one of my servants will be my heir." Then the Lord said to him, "No, your servant will not be your heir, for you will have a son of your own who will be your heir." Then the Lord took Abram outside and said to him, "Look up into the sky and count the stars if you can. That's how many descendants you will have!" And Abram believed the Lord, and the Lord counted him as righteous because of his faith. (Genesis 15:1–6 NLT)

In Genesis 12 (from the previous text), God promised to make Abram (Abraham) into a great nation. Without knowing where he was going, Abram believed (trusted) God and stepped out on faith. "Faith is the confidence that what we hope for will actually happen; it gives us assurance about things we cannot see" (Hebrews 11:1 NLT).

Abram did not conform to the standards of worship/idolatry that most of his family and countrymen in the land of Haran practiced. Although his family knew of God and his divinity, most of them chose to continue living sinful lifestyles. Fortunately a few of these people, including Abram, earnestly sought to follow God. How many of you know that in this modern day, we must not flow with the majority. Even today the majority seeks to live sinful lifestyles. When we choose to obey and follow God through Jesus Christ, we are among the few just like Abram.

Sure, there are many who attend worship services at the local churches, and many who say they are Christians. But how many are really living for God? Not a lifestyle of perfection on the human scale but a lifestyle of pleasing God by faith in Christ (believing and obeying his instructions for your life). By faith, we become sons of God. "For you are all children of God through faith in Christ Jesus" (Galatians 3:26 NLT). What separates us from the majority is our faith (trusting and obeying God). Genesis 15:6 (NLT) says, "And Abram believed the Lord, and the Lord counted him as righteous because of his faith." Through faith we are counted as righteous in the eyes of God. We get God's attention when we turn our heart to him and when we believe he is who he says he is.

How many of you want to be in the will of God? Not to be lived every now and then, but you want to make it your lifestyle, your way of living. In Christ, we are not our own. We have been bought with the price of his blood. It is not up us to make our own decisions. By faith we give ourselves to Christ and allow his Spirit to be our guide in life. The Word of God also tells us that the righteous shall live by faith (see Hebrews 10:38).

As Abram journeyed, he trusted and obeyed God's instructions. God, who also trusted Abram, continued to commune with him as their covenant relationship blossomed. As a sign of their covenant, God changed Abram's name to Abraham and blessed him and his household. Abraham was seventy-five years old and had no children when God originally came to him concerning the promise of making him into a great nation, and at the age of one hundred, Abraham gave birth to Isaac, his promised son. For twenty-five years, Abraham trusted God for the promise. I would have to believe that before his encounter with God, his faith was the size of a mustard seed; however, through persistence and perseverance, he overcame many obstacles and tests, and God took him to new levels in his faith.

How many of you today are living life on purpose and believe God for what he promised you some years ago. One of the most fascinating things about your life in Christ is believing God for his promise(s) and trusting he will lead you right into your destiny. Is your life lined up or lining up with the promises of God?

When we believe God for the things hoped for, we are walking by faith. If you know what God has spoken to you, you must keep trusting, believing, and walking in obedience unto God. Even when it does not look like it will come to pass, keep believing, for we walk by faith, not by sight (2 Corinthians 5:7 KJV).

The Spiritual Gift of Faith Is an Extraordinary Trust in God

First Corinthians 12 gives us a short list of spiritual gifts given by the Holy Spirit.

> Now there are varieties of gifts, but the same Spirit. And there are varieties of ministries, and the same Lord. There are varieties of effects, but the same God who works all things in all persons. But to each one is given the manifestation of the Spirit for the common good. For to one is given the word of wisdom through the Spirit, and to another the word of knowledge according to the same Spirit; to another faith by the same Spirit, and to another gifts of healing by the one Spirit, and to another the effecting of miracles, and to another prophecy, and to another the distinguishing of spirits, to another various kinds of tongues, and to another the interpretation of tongues. But one and the same Spirit works all these things, distributing to each one individually just as He wills. (1 Corinthians 12:4–11 NASB)

We become Christians when we choose from the heart to trust and believe (have faith) in God through Jesus Christ (see Romans 10:9–10). In the previous Scripture, we learn that faith is also a spiritual gift given by the Holy Spirit. You may think, *As Christians, we all already have faith. Why is faith a spiritual gift?* Yes, we (Christians) all have faith, but the Holy Spirit also gives a spiritual gift of faith. The spiritual gift of faith is an extraordinary dose of trust in the power and sovereignty of the almighty God.

Those with the spiritual gift of faith have such an extraordinary trust in the Lord, their God, that they are willing to let go of their lives and submit themselves completely to the lordship of Jesus Christ. They trust and believe wholeheartedly in all that God is (all-powerful, all-knowing, righteous, just, faithful, unfailing love, etc.), and there is nothing he can't do. They confidently believe that all things are possible with God (see Mark 10:27).

Jesus's extraordinary Trust in God

> Then Jesus was led by the Spirit into the wilderness to be tempted by the devil. After fasting forty days and forty nights, he was hungry. The tempter came to him and said, "If you are the Son of God, tell these stones to become bread." Jesus answered, "It is written: 'Man does not live on bread alone, but on every word that comes from the mouth of God.

Then the devil took him to the holy city and had him stand on the highest point of the temple. "If you are the Son of God," he said, "throw yourself down. For it is written: '"He will command his angels concerning you, and they will lift you up in their hands, so that you will not strike your foot against a stone. Jesus answered him, "It is also written: 'Do not put the Lord your God to the test.' Again, the devil took him to a very high mountain and showed him all the kingdoms of the world and their splendor. "All this I will give you," he said, "if you will bow down and worship me." Jesus said to him, "Away from me, Satan! For it is written: 'Worship the Lord your God, and serve him only.' Then the devil left him, and angels came and attended him. (Matthew 4:1–11 NIV)

Jesus is our perfect example of one who, in the flesh, had an extraordinary trust in God to carry out his God-given assignment. We begin to see his trust and obedience to God just before he began his ministry when he was willing to be led by the Holy Spirit into the wilderness for an extended period of time. Jesus was obedient to God's call for a dry fast (no food or water). Once in the wilderness, he faced difficult times of testing and trials by the Devil. Jesus, being grounded in the knowledge of God's Word, was victorious over the temptations of the Devil. The Devil, who was also knowledgeable in the Word of God, used it to tempt Jesus by misinterpreting and twisting its meaning. Jesus trusted and obeyed the truth of God's Word over the tempting requests of the Devil.

At what level do you trust God with your life? I'm sure you are more than willing to allow the Spirit of God to lead you beside the still waters, but what about in the paths of righteousness for his name's sake? Are you willing to trust God with a heart to do what is morally right by obeying the truth of his Word? What about when the fires of your trials become seven times hotter. Are you willing to trust God while journeying through the valley of the shadow of death? His Word says in Psalm 23:4, "I shall fear no evil, for you (God) are with me."

Jesus trusted wholeheartedly in the Holy Spirit's mighty power upon him to preach the gospel to the poor, to heal the brokenhearted, to preach deliverance to the captives, to recover sight for the blind, to set at liberty those who are bruised, and to declare that the time of the Lord's favor has come (see Luke 4:18–19).

Do you trust the Spirit of God to lead you on the journey to your purpose? The journey may be long. It may be strenuous. You may have to endure some great tests and trials. Every road will not be straight, and every day will not be perfect and sunny. But those who endure to the end and wait on the Lord will arrive at their season of purpose, blessed by God to move out in that God-given assignment. Just as he did with Jesus, the Spirit of the Lord shall come upon you (in God's timing), anointing you to do his great work in the earth. Jesus said in John 14:12 (NIV), "I tell you the truth, anyone who has faith in me will do what I have been doing. He will do even greater things than these, because I am going to the Father."

Trusting God even unto Death

When God created mankind (Adam and Eve), he created them in his own image and placed them in the garden of Eden, a beautiful garden full of life where all their needs would be met. God gave mankind specific instructions for taking care of the garden and caring of themselves. God forbade mankind from eating the fruit from the Tree of Knowledge of Good and Evil; however, through temptation, mankind disobeyed God's instruction and ate of the fruit. This one act of sin (disobedience) brought the curse of death into the world, and all of Adam and Eve's descendants (mankind) were cursed unto death.

Death is our final enemy, yet Jesus conquered death through his resurrection. When God wrapped himself in flesh (in the form of man) and came into the world, he came with divine purpose, and that purpose was for the benefit of all humanity. He did this so that humanity might be redeemed from a fate of sin and death and brought back into a relationship with God the Father and receive eternal life. Jesus came so that we may see, know, and experience God for ourselves. Jesus trusted and believed God for his God-given assignment in the earth. He was perfect and without sin, yet he took on the punishment for our sins. Through his ministry on earth, he was obedient to God all the way to his death on the cross. Jesus exemplified extreme humility, trust, submission, and obedience unto God when he allowed himself to be wounded for our transgressions and bruised for our iniquities and when he bore the punishment that brought us peace. His finished work on the cross is more than enough to satisfy our every need and to remove every burden we may be carrying.

I challenge you to go before God in prayer and ask for increased faith, guidance, and understanding concerning your divine purpose/assignment. As you can see, we (mankind) mirror our maker. Just like Christ, we were not created and put here on earth for selfish reasons but for selfless reasons. Christ came and gave his life (a selfless deed) for our sake.

After all he has done, are you willing to adjust your attitude to one of gratitude for his unconditional acts of love and grace given to you as a free gift? Can you now trust him with all your heart and submit to your God-given assignment, allowing him to lead you through to the end? How far are you willing to trust God during the journey? If you trust God, what pain and sufferings are you willing to go through out of obedience to him for the sake of others? What sacrifices are you willing to make for the sake of others?

Do you believe in the power of God? Do you trust and believe that he came to earth in the flesh to die for the sins of this world? Do you believe that he was resurrected after he died and was buried so that we could be restored back into fellowship with God, receiving and sharing in eternal life with Christ? Do you believe that he did that for us?

Do you trust in that same power that raised Jesus from the dead to quicken your mortal body to life as well?

CHAPTER 4

Love

Have you given your whole self for God as he has given his whole self for you? He proved his love for us when he gave all he had on the cross. Many people say, "I love you," but really they have no earthly idea what they are stating. *I love you* is a statement used very loosely and without understanding of the true meaning of love. The Bible tells us that God is love (1 John 4:8), so to understand love, we need to look to God. Love was not created. Love has always existed.

Most people generally describe love as an adoring fondness or warmth for another person, a sexual passion, or a feeling of emotional and personal attachment toward someone or something. This may then explain why the term *love* is used loosely throughout society. While these descriptions are fitting for the world, we must take a deeper dive into what it means to love, especially since it is a command from God.

> One of the teachers of the law came and heard them debating. Noticing that Jesus had given them a good answer, he asked him, "Of all the

commandments, which is the most important?" "The most important one," answered Jesus, "is this: 'Hear, O Israel, the Lord our God, the Lord is one. Love the Lord your God with all your heart and with all your soul and with all your mind and with all your strength.' The second is this: 'Love your neighbor as yourself.' There is no commandment greater than these." "Well said, teacher," the man replied. "You are right in saying that God is one and there is no other but him. To love him with all your heart, with all your understanding and with all your strength, and to love your neighbor as yourself is more important than all burnt offerings and sacrifices." When Jesus saw that he had answered wisely, he said to him, "You are not far from the kingdom of God." And from then on no one dared ask him any more questions. (Mark 12:28–34 NIV)

Jesus teaches us that our first and greatest command is to love the Lord, our God, with all of our heart, with all of our soul, with all of our mind, and with all of our strength. These four components (heart, soul, mind, and strength) are the very essence of our entire being. Jesus immediately followed up with the second command, "Love your neighbor as yourself," which is greatly related (in manner of love) to the first command of love for God. Not only does he command us to love him, but we are also supposed to love others with the same kind of love. Our unconditional love toward him opens our heart to unconditionally love for others. Can you see the reflection of his image shining through this command? God commands us to love because he loves. Love is who he is.

When God gave the children of Israel the Ten Commandments, the first commandment given stated, "You shall have no other gods before me" (Exodus 20:3 NIV). Through the Ten Commandments, God gave the terms (the Law) he required in order for the children of Israel to enter and remain in a covenant relationship with him, a life of holiness. A covenant relationship with God requires commitment and discipline. If you can commit yourself to fulfilling God's law of love by loving him and him alone, then the discipline of loving and caring for others should become part of your very nature. Loving God brings out God's love in you, causing you to reflect his love toward others.

For many years I sought to get understanding of what true love really means. I brought up the topic of love with a few friends, and I could not get a satisfying answer. Some didn't say much at all while others (the know-it-alls) responded with answers so far off the mark that they vexed my soul with their answers. Well, it dawned on me one day. If I want pure wisdom and understanding, I must get it from God.

Through prayer and meditation, I asked the Lord to give me wisdom concerning the meaning of true love. One of the first things God began speaking into my spirit was this: "For God so loved the world, that he gave his only begotten Son" (see John 3:16 KJV). I sat quietly in my prayer room and thought, *Wow, for God so loved the world that he gave—* Still thinking about what He was saying to me, I immediately began to understand that love is about giving. From there he led me to 1 John 3:16 (NLT), which says, "We know what real love is because Jesus gave up his life for us. So we also ought to give up our lives for our brothers and sisters." I was completely amazed by the wisdom and understanding I received from those two verses alone. I continued to read through to the end of chapter 3 (verses 17–24), and in receiving this Word, my life changed forever. I had an incredible aha moment. Though I had read these passages many times before, understanding God's deep love for mankind, the revelation I received at that moment was that his action was the perfect example of the meaning of true love.

Jesus, the Son of God, who was God, gave all he had out of love. He gave even his life for the sake of others. He then earnestly urged his followers to do the same for one another.

> We know what real love is because Jesus gave up his life for us. So we also ought to give up our lives for our brothers and sisters. If someone has enough money to live well and sees a brother or sister in need but shows no compassion—how can God's love be in that person? Dear children, let's not merely say that we love each other; let us show the truth by our actions. Our actions will show that we belong to the truth, so we will be confident when we stand before God. Even if we feel guilty, God is greater than our feelings, and he knows everything. Dear friends, if we don't feel guilty, we can come to God with bold confidence. And we will receive from him whatever we ask because we obey him and do the things that please him. And this is his commandment: We must believe in the name of his Son, Jesus Christ, and love one another, just as he commanded us. Those who obey God's commandments remain

in fellowship with him, and he with them. And
we know he lives in us because the Spirit he gave
us lives in us. (1 John 3:16–24 NLT)

Is your heart conditioned for such love as this? Has your mind been renewed and transformed for such love as this? Are you willing to love from the core of your soul? And finally, are you willing to give up your life for the sake of others? This kind of love generates sacrificial giving. To give up one's life does not always or necessarily mean physical death. But what it does call for is the crucifying of our flesh (dying to our own selfish want or gain) for the sake of others. By faith we may need to give up our time for a season to assist Christian brothers or sisters with their God-given assignments. By faith we may need to give up our own resources for the sake of other people's needs. By faith we may actually need to give up our lives (death) for the sake of sparing others. We must give that same godly love that God has for us to others through our actions. Benevolence is born out of this kind of love. This true love is charity at its best.

"The Greatest of These Is Charity (Love)"

In several passages of the New Testament, the King James Version of the Holy Bible uses the word *charity* in place of the word *love*. The Greek word for charity in these New Testament occurrences is *agape*.[4] The term *agape* can mean "having an unconditional love toward someone or others." Agape love is unselfish, giving, and a genuine concern for the health and welfare of humanity.

---

4   This term is referenced from the *New Strong's Exhaustive Concordance of the Bible* copyright © 1990 by Thomas Nelson Publishers, Greek 26.

In 1 Corinthians 13, we will find practically an entire chapter on the attributes of true love. What is so significant about this real kind of love that the apostle Paul found it necessary to write about in his first letter to the Corinthian church, making certain they understood that the greatest gift one could possess was (and still is) love?

> If I speak in the tongues of men and of angels, but have not love, I am only a resounding gong or a clanging cymbal. If I have the gift of prophecy and can fathom all mysteries and all knowledge, and if I have a faith that can move mountains, but have not love, I am nothing. If I give all I possess to the poor and surrender my body to the flames, but have not love, I gain nothing. Love is patient, love is kind. It does not envy, it does not boast, it is not proud. It is not rude, it is not self-seeking, it is not easily angered, it keeps no record of wrongs. Love does not delight in evil but rejoices with the truth. It always protects, always trusts, always hopes, always perseveres. Love never fails. But where there are prophecies, they will cease; where there are tongues, they will be stilled; where there is knowledge, it will pass away. For we know in part and we prophesy in part, but when perfection comes, the imperfect disappears. When I was a child, I talked like a child, I thought like a child, I reasoned like a child. When I became a man, I put childish ways behind me. Now we see but a poor reflection as in a mirror; then we shall see face to face. Now

I know in part; then I shall know fully, even as
I am fully known. And now these three remain:
faith, hope and love. But the greatest of these is
love. (1 Corinthians 13:1–13 NIV)

In order for us to understand the reason for Paul's motivation to teach and describe the characteristics of true love in chapter 13, we will need to know some background about the Corinthian church.

The Christians at Corinth had several issues and questions concerning Christianity (living for Christ) that needed addressing. One of the issues concerned spiritual gifts. Instead of their spiritual gifts being used for building up and unifying the church, they were misusing them and allowing them to become symbols of power (i.e., who has the greatest and/or better spiritual power).

In chapter 12, Paul teaches the Corinthians that there are many different kinds of spiritual gifts but that they all are given by the same Spirit. Spiritual gifts are special abilities given by the Holy Spirit for the purpose of ministering to the needs of fellow Christian brothers and sisters and not for our own selfish purpose and reasons. Paul explains that just as there is one human body with many members (see 1 Corinthians 12:12), the same is true with us as believers in Christ. We (believers) are the one body in Christ. Christ is the head of his body, and his body has many members (the believers). He further explains that just as the human body has many members (hands, fingers, toes, legs, feet, arms, heart, liver, etc.) that perform various functions, working harmoniously together for the created purpose of the human body, no member was better than another, and he also stated that no member could survive on their own without the assistance of the others. The same is said for the body of Christ. The body of Christ has many members (diverse groups of people with various gifts given by the Holy Spirit) that perform various functions, all working harmoniously together for the perfecting of one another and bringing unity within Christ's body of believers. No spiritual gift is more superior than another. "They were given to us for serving God and enhancing the spiritual growth of the body of believers."[5]

Paul strongly encourages us to understand that while spiritual gifts are very important, the greatest gift that we can possess is love. Although people have different spiritual gifts, love is available to everyone. Remember, love is expressed through one's actions and not by words and emotional feelings alone.

God wrapped himself in flesh and came to earth and dwelled among us. Through the life of Jesus Christ, we (humanity) came to know God and his love for humanity. Jesus says, "I am the way, the truth, and the life. No one can come to the Father except through me" (John 14:6 NLT). Through wholeheartedly accepting Christ as your Lord and Savior for his selfless work on the cross and living a life dedicated to Christ, you will find yourself a living expression of God that is pleasing in the eyes of God himself.

---

[5] *Notes and Bible Helps* copyright © 1988, 1989, 1990, 1991, 1993, 1996 by Tyndale House Publishers, Inc. All rights reserved. Used by Permission of Tyndale House Publishers, Inc.

For everyone who truly loves God, the love of God (as described in 1 Corinthians 13) is in them and manifests through their actions in life. Let us look at the life of love that Christ demonstrated for us.

Love is patient (1 Corinthians 13:4 NIV).
Christ demonstrates patience with us daily. Whether we are followers of Christ or dead in sin, Christ's love for humanity is evident as he demonstrates patience through his grace and mercy. Jesus was patient with his disciples as he taught them and shared knowledge about the kingdom of God. Throughout the gospels we see the times when the disciples did not grasp the mysteries and parables Jesus spoke about, but Jesus did not condemn them. Instead he continued speaking through a spirit of love to help them to grasp and understand. How many times are we ready to throw the baby out with the bathwater when someone we are training does not grasp the information the first time? Jesus knew we were more to him than our faults or deficiencies. Further, Jesus demonstrated patience with those who were yet sinners. As Jesus was teaching at the temple, the scribes and the Pharisees brought a woman who had been caught in the act of adultery, and they put her in front of the crowd (see John 8:3). They explained to him that the woman was caught in the act of adultery and that the law of Moses said that such a person should be stoned to death. Jesus recognized that

they were attempting to trick him into doing or saying something against the law, so instead Jesus patiently handled the situation by returning a question to them, thereby saving the sinner from further judgment and condemnation and saving himself from their false accusations. He patiently took the time to speak out of love to the woman, encouraging her to go and sin no more.

Love is kind (1 Corinthians 13:4 NIV).
The life and ministry of Jesus Christ was filled with random acts of kindness. He healed the sick, caused the dumb to speak and the lame to walk, set captives free, caused the dead to rise, delivered good news to the poor, etc. However, he expected nothing in return. Christ demonstrated great kindness when he looked upon the multitude of his followers with compassion. His disciples sought to send them all home to their villages so that they could buy food for themselves, but Jesus thought differently. He told the disciples that sending them away would not be necessary and commanded that they should feed the multitude. Although there were only five loaves of bread and two fish, Jesus made a way so that they could feed more than five thousand people. Jesus recognized and did not waste or mishandle his God- given gift of working miracles. Kindness comes from a heart filled with love and compassion for the welfare of others.

Love does not envy (1 Corinthians 13:4 NIV).
Through a pure heart of love, Jesus advocates for God's children. Seated at the right hand of God and interceding on our behalf, Jesus demonstrates that he is praying for us and not against us. Most of us at some point in our lives have or will experience meeting people who say they are our friends, but in time we discover that they were never really for us. With their hearts filled with envy and their motives impure, it turns out that all along they were against us. This is not the case with Jesus. He is righteous. We can take him at his Word that we have a true friend in him. Who else but Jesus Christ would see to it that we, the children of God, become joint heirs of the kingdom with him? No envy and jealousy can be found in his heart.

**Love does not boast, and it is not proud
(1 Corinthians 13:4 NIV).**
Out of pure love for humanity, Christ humbled himself and came to earth in the form of a human for our sake. Paul encourages believers in Philippians 2 to have the same mind- set as Jesus Christ "Who, being in very nature God, did not consider equality with God something to be grasped, but made himself nothing by, taking the very nature of a servant, being made in human likeness. And being found in appearance as a man, he humbled himself and became obedient to death—even death on a cross" (Philippians

2:6–8 NIV)! Here we have Christ in the form of God (with supernatural power). He had the perfect opportunity to brag and boast about such power, but godly love did not allow him to think twice about himself. Instead he cared more about the human soul. He demonstrated humility by lowering himself to a place of servanthood to serve God in the form of a human being with extreme obedience and determination to complete his work on the cross.

Love does not behave rudely
(1 Corinthians 13:5 NKJV).

It was not on his heart to snub the Samaritan woman when she came to the well, but instead Jesus demonstrated love through offering up a warm, friendly conversation. He did not allow cultural constraints and the hateful opinions of the Jews toward the Samarians stop him from talking with the woman (see John 4:1–26). He continued to be about his Father's business by loving others regardless of race, color, religion, ethnicity, etc.

Love is not always "me first"
(1 Corinthians 13:5 MSG).

Jesus made it quite clear in his discussion with the sons of Zebedee and their mother that the Son of Man came not to be served but to serve (see Matthew 20:28). His purpose for coming to the earth was to redeem humanity from sin and death in exchange for the ransom of his own life.

He demonstrated love in the highest degree by literally putting the lives of humanity in front of his own life. Throughout his ministry, he sought not to be served by others, but rather he served them. Jesus displayed the attitude of a model servant, putting others first, when he stooped to the level of the lowliest of servants and washed the feet of his disciples (see John 13:1–17). The disciples were stunned at this great act of humility expressed by their Lord and Master.

**Love is not easily angered
(1 Corinthians 13:5 NIV).**
In Jesus's Sermon on the Mount (Matthew 5–7), he opens with teaching his followers the beatitudes, which I call "a Christian believer's code of conduct." This entire assembly of beatitudes is all-inclusive, and it is not about picking and choosing your behavioral standards from the list. As a Christian believer, your behavior must reflect these moral values as a whole. Nestled right in the heart of these values, it says, "Blessed are the peace-makers, for they shall be called the children of God." Peace reconciles relationships while anger destroys relationships. Christ demonstrated the spirit of peacemaking when he reconciled humanity's relationship back to God through his selfless act on the cross.

Love keeps no record of wrongs (1 Corinthians 13:5 NIV).

Forgiveness comes right from the heart of God. Jesus kept no record of our wrongs when he saw to it that our sins were washed away by his blood, giving us a new life in him. Romans 5:8 (NLT) says, "But God showed his great love for us by sending Christ to die for us while we were still sinners." The key in this verse is "while we were still sinners," meaning that he knew we were sinners but that his love for us overshadowed the wrongs of our past and made way for our victorious future in Christ. Throughout Jesus's ministry, he demonstrated love that keeps no record of wrongs when he forgave an adulterer, a prostitute, and a murderer and healed many who were sick. Their pasts have been forgotten. The willingness to forgive demonstrates love that keeps no record of wrongs.

Love does not delight in evil but rejoices with the truth (1 Corinthians 13:6 NIV).

Through the heart of God, just as love keeps no record of our sins, so does love not rejoice in our sin. Jesus does not rejoice in our lowest point in life, but instead he did something about it. He gave his own life. When the lame person lay on his bed and had been there for years, Jesus didn't sit and rejoice in this man's misfortune. Instead he spoke a word of power and truth, "Get up and walk," and the man walked.

Love always protects (1 Corinthians 13:7 NIV).
As a father protects his child, so does God the Father protect us. Jesus demonstrates his love and protection daily by interceding on our behalf. Jesus promises we will have everlasting care and protection even after he returns back to the Father in heaven. He explained to his disciples in John 14:16 (KJV), "And I will pray the Father, and he shall give you another Comforter, that he may abide with you forever."

Love always trusts (1 Corinthians 13:7 NIV).
To trust means to possess a level of faith in someone or a situation. Jesus demonstrates great trust in his disciples to follow after his teachings and to do as he has commanded, namely to love one another. He has entrusted his disciples to impart his love to others by giving our lives for them as he gave his life for us. Those who love are not suspicious of the ones they love. They trust first in what is lovely and pure about others, and they are slow to believe what is ugly and impure about people. Through Christ's command to love one another, we trust in his help and guidance as we affect change in the earth.

Love always hopes (1 Corinthians 13:7 NIV).
Through loving others, we can bring a sense of hope to their lives just as Christ's love brought hope to all believers. Our believing in Christ (our faith) makes us confident that what we hope for

will actually happen. It gives us assurance about things we cannot see. We are the light of Christ in this dark and hopeless world, and through loving others, we bring Christ to them, which helps them have confidence that what they hope for will actually happen. Love brings hope to hopeless situations.

Love always perseveres (1 Corinthians 13:7 NIV). Out of complete and unconditional love for humankind, Christ endured all the way to the cross. Love allowed him to endure our punishment for sin even unto death. He persevered through every bruise, every cut, every nail, every utter of persecution for the sake of humanity. Regardless of our circumstances, believers possessing godly love endure and persevere through the challenges in life and remain committed to the work of the Lord.

Love never fails (1 Corinthians 13:8 NIV). God is love (1 John 4:8), and if our eternal God is love, then love is eternal (never-ending) as well. God's unfailing love for us is revealed to us through Moses in Deuteronomy 31:6 (NIV). Moses encourages Israel to "be strong and courageous. Do not be afraid or terrified because of them, for the Lord your God goes with you; he will never leave you nor forsake you." God's unfaltering and unfailing love is also revealed through the apostle Paul when he said, "And I am convinced that nothing can ever separate us from God's love. Neither death nor life, neither angels nor demons, neither our fears for today nor our worries about tomorrow—not even the powers of hell can separate us from God's love. No power in the sky above or in the earth below—indeed, nothing in all creation will ever be able to separate us from the love of God that is revealed in Christ Jesus our Lord" (Romans 8:38–39 NLT).

Love God—Love Others

I have loved you even as the Father has loved me. Remain in my love. When you obey my commandments, you remain in my love, just as I obey my Father's commandments and remain in his love. I have told you these things so that you will be filled with my joy. Yes, your joy will overflow! This is my commandment: Love each other in the same way I have loved you. There is no greater love than to lay down one's life for one's friends. You are my friends if you do what I command. I no longer call you slaves, because a master doesn't confide in his slaves. Now you are my friends, since I have told you everything the Father told me. You didn't choose me. I chose you. I appointed you to go and produce lasting fruit, so that the Father will give you whatever you ask for, using my name. This is my command: Love each other. (John 15:9–17 NLT)

Our greatest command is to love. The greatest gift we can possess is love. When we choose to obey our Lord's commandments and take on this kind of unconditional godly love for Christ and for others, we remain in the love and favor of our Lord and Savior. Our covenant relationship blossoms in love at an optimum and trustworthy capacity.

Have you taken the time to display true love to someone today? This week? This month? Have you unselfishly given your time, resources, and/or talents for the sake of others?

These questions remind me of how even the smallest acts of love can brighten and encourage the hearts of many people, affecting change across communities, cities, states, and nations.

Last Christmas season I went to the mall to pick up a few gifts for my daughters. As I was leaving the mall, I noticed a booth set up for the Salvation Army. I walked over to the table and asked the young man if they were taking donations. He pointed down at a very small container on the table and said, "Yes, you can put your cash donation in here." He went on to explain that the booth is primarily set up for the "Angel Tree." As I looked up, I saw that just behind the booth there was a Christmas tree with neatly arranged tags containing the age and gender of a child and the child's Christmas wish. I remembered participating in a similar program a few years back, and although I was aware of the Angel Tree, I had not participated in this particular program. The young man invited me to come behind the booth and pick a child from the tree. When I got to the tree, I decided to choose one boy and one girl. I received the instructions and deadline to have the gifts back to the mall. Then I turned to leave.

As I walked past the booth, the Holy Spirit said, "Go get more kids," when I heard this, I immediately obeyed the still, small voice in my heart, turned, and went back to the tree.

I explained to the young man, "I need to get more kids."

He had no complaints and said, "Please … help yourself," and I pulled a few more children from the Angel Tree.

When I arrived at my car and began to drive away, my heart was filled because I knew that giving was a display of love and was a blessing to the lives of those in need. God was well pleased with this kind of love I was showing others, and his Spirit fell on me so mightily that I began to cry. I pulled over in the mall parking lot to allow God to have his way with me. I prayed and thanked God for being in my life and for blessing me so that I could bless others. True love is not self-seeking. True love seeks ways to bless the lives of others. As you can see, even when we display the smallest acts of love toward others, God makes his presence known in the relationship. He lets us know that we are in this relationship together, and he sees your unselfish expression of love toward others.

- If you love God, you will fear him (with great reverence).
- If you love God, you will trust him.
- If you love God, you will obey him.
- If you love God, you will submit to him.

- If you love God, you will humble yourself before him.
- If you love God, you will wait on him.
- If you say you love God, then you are also saying you have given up your own will for your life and have given it over to him so that he may use you according to his will and for the benefit of others.

CHAPTER 5

Submission

Oftentimes submission is a topic feared, overlooked, and/or not even discussed. I believe the topic of submission is feared primarily because it requires one giving over his or her very own will. Although submission is a key requirement in any healthy relationship, many people view submission as a sign of weakness in a person. In order for a relationship to be affective, all persons involved must submit to the reception of communication from the other(s). No one person's voice or ideas should be so important that others are never allowed to speak. If so, that relationship can soon become very toxic. Even in our relationship with God, communication is not one-sided. It is a healthy two-way conversation with us and God.

In chapter 2, we discussed God's desire for intimate fellowship with us. He welcomes us to express our thoughts and concerns with him daily. God loves and respects his children. Therefore, even he submits himself to be attentive to our prayers and supplication. Submission is not a sign of weakness; it is a sign of love and trust. If we love God and trust him for who he is, we can then submit to his mighty power and authority.

What is so important about submission that it makes the list of moral values to adhere to in living a holy life for God? In this chapter on submission, we are referring to the act of giving over or surrendering ourselves to the will, power, or authority of another. Submission is an internal attitude that comes from our heart, and since we are given free will to choose our own way and actions for our lives, then it is ours to choose whether we will submit to God's power and authority or not. As a child should submit to the authority of his or her parents, so shall we submit to the power and authority (the will) of God through Christ.

God commands all children, regardless of age or status, to honor and obey their earthly father and mother. This command lets us realize that parents have a special place in the eyes of God. The honoring of parents is so important to God that it is one of the Ten Commandments. "Honor your father and mother. Then you will live a long, full life in the land the Lord your God is giving you (Exodus 20:12 NLT). The apostle Paul reiterates this commandment in Ephesians 6:1–3. He also explains that this is the first commandment with a promise attached. To those who honor their father and mother, God promises a long and fulfilled life of peace. God also makes this same promise of a long and fulfilled life to those who choose to submit to his power and authority (see Deuteronomy 30:19–20). Our decision whether to honor and respect God the Father by submitting to his power and authority is a matter of life or death, so choose life!

Submitting to the Will of God

In our covenant relationship with God, submitting to his will is more than just honor and respect. It is an act of totally surrendering the self and will with all one's heart, soul, mind, and strength. Just as we are to love God with all of our heart, soul, mind, and strength (see Mark 12:29), we must surrender ourselves to him with this same passion. Surrendering or giving up ourselves at this level requires wholehearted confidence and trust in God. In chapter 3, we discussed trusting God. If we are going to walk in a covenant relationship with God, we will need to trust him. Without trusting God, we will never be able to surrender ourselves and our will to him.

Who Is God?

Who is God that we are better off submitting to his will as opposed to our own will? Who is God to each of us personally that we can put 100 percent trust in him and submit to his will even as Christ did? As Jesus Christ agonized in the garden, knowing his suffering that lie ahead, he prayed to the Father and asked, "O my Father, if it be possible, let this cup pass from me: nevertheless not as I will, but as thou wilt" (Matthew 26:39 KJV). Perhaps we can find the answer by taking a closer look at God's attributes and who he is to us personally.

Attributes of God

We could write forever and not cover the endless attributes or characteristics of God, but for the sake of achieving insight into the reason for choosing God's will over our own, we will highlight a few of God's awesome attributes. These attributes will help us to further grasp the vastness and greatness of God, thereby making our decision to surrender to his will a comforting choice.

God Is Creator

> In the beginning God created the heavens and the earth. Now the earth was formless and empty, darkness was over the surface of the deep, and the Spirit of God was hovering over the waters. And God said, "Let there be light," and there was light. God saw that the light was good, and he separated the light from the darkness. God called the light "day," and the darkness he called "night." And there was evening, and there was morning—the first day. And God said, "Let there be an expanse between the waters to separate water from water." So God made the expanse and separated the water under the expanse from the water above it. And it was so. God called the expanse "sky." And there was evening, and there was morning—the second day. And God said, "Let the water under the sky be gathered to one place, and let dry ground appear." And it was so. God called the dry ground "land," and the gathered waters he called "seas."

And God saw that it was good. Then God said, "Let the land produce vegetation: seed-bearing plants and trees on the land that bear fruit with seed in it, according to their various kinds." And it was so. The land produced vegetation: plants bearing seed according to their kinds and trees bearing fruit with seed in it according to their kinds. And God saw that it was good. And there was evening, and there was morning—the third day. And God said, "Let there be lights in the expanse of the sky to separate the day from the night, and let them serve as signs to mark seasons, and days and years, and let them be lights in the expanse of the sky to give light on the earth." And it was so. God made two great lights—the greater light to govern the day and the lesser light to govern the night. He also made the stars. God set them in the expanse of the sky to give light on the earth, to govern the day and the night, and to separate light from darkness. And God saw that it was good. And there was evening, and there was morning—the fourth day. And God said, "Let the water teem with living creatures, and let birds fly above the earth across the expanse of the sky." So God created the great creatures of the sea and every living and moving thing with which the water teems, according to their kinds, and every winged bird according to its kind. And God saw that it was good. God blessed them and said, "Be fruitful and increase in number and fill the water in the seas, and let the birds increase on the earth." And there was evening, and there was morning—the fifth day. And God said, "Let the land produce living creatures according to their kinds: the livestock, the creatures that move along the ground, and wild animals, each according to its kind." And it was so. God made the wild animals according to their kinds, the livestock according to their kinds, and all the creatures that move along the ground according to their kinds. And God saw that it was good. Then God said, "Let us make man in our image, in our likeness, and let them rule over the fish of the sea and the birds of the air, over the livestock, over all the earth, and over all the creatures that move along the ground." So God created man in his own image, in the image of God he created him; male and female he created them. God blessed them and said to them, "Be fruitful and increase in number; fill the earth and subdue it. Rule over the fish of the sea and the birds of the air and over every living creature that moves on the ground." Then God said, "I give you every seed-bearing plant on the face of the whole earth and every tree that has fruit with seed in it. They will be yours for food. And to all the beasts of the earth and all the birds of the air and all the creatures that move along the ground—everything that has the breath of life in it—I give every green plant for food." And it was so. God saw all that he had made, and it was very good. And there was evening, and there was morning—the sixth day. (Genesis 1:1–31 NIV)

Thus the heavens and the earth were completed in all their vast array. By the seventh day God had finished the work he had been doing; so on the seventh day he rested from all his work. And God blessed the seventh day and made it holy, because on it he rested from all the work of creating that he had done. (Genesis 2:1–3 NIV)

The Holy Bible, our manual of truth, clearly informs us in the first chapter of the first book that God is the Creator of the heavens and the earth and all that is within the heavens and earth. How the universe and the earth came into existence has been an age-old debate for centuries. But frankly the *how* isn't nearly as important as the *who*. I don't doubt that there were big bangs and collisions, but there is only one Creator who has the power to bring such perfection together to create the universe and all that is within it. God is not only Creator, but he is also all-powerful, all-knowing, and sovereign.

God Is All-Powerful. God Is All-Knowing. God Is Sovereign.

In the text to follow, God spoke to Job, asking him a series of questions. God's questions to Job open our eyes to his great power, knowledge, and sovereignty. There is none like him and none even worthy of questioning his decisions. Who is able to stand with God and match his power, wisdom, knowledge, and understanding? Job 11:7–8 (NLT) says, "Can you solve the mysteries of God? Can you discover everything about the Almighty? Such knowledge is higher than the heavens—and who are you? It is deeper than the underworld—what do you know?" With his great power and might, he laid the foundations of the earth. He determined its measurements and knows the complete extent of the earth and everything in it. He is our almighty God, who set forth the rhythmic movements of the entire universe (times, seasons, spheres, and cycles).

Then the Lord spoke to Job out of the storm. He said: "Who is this that darkens my counsel with words without knowledge? Brace yourself like a man; I will question you, and you shall answer me. "Where were you when I laid the earth's foundation? Tell me, if you understand. Who marked off its dimensions? Surely you know! Who stretched a measuring line across it? On what were its footings set, or who laid its cornerstone—while the morning stars sang together and all the angels shouted for joy? "Who shut up the sea behind doors when it burst forth from the womb, when I made the clouds its garment and wrapped it in thick darkness, when I fixed limits for it and set its doors and bars in place, when I said, 'This far you may come and no farther; here is where your proud waves halt'? "Have you ever given orders to the morning, or shown the dawn its place, that it might take the earth by the edges and shake the wicked out of it? The earth takes shape like clay under a seal; its features stand out like those of a garment. The wicked are denied their light, and their upraised arm is broken. "Have you journeyed to the springs of the sea or walked in the recesses of the deep? Have the gates of death been shown to you? Have you seen the gates of the shadow of death? Have you comprehended the vast expanses of the earth? Tell me, if you know all this. "What is the way to the abode of light? And where does darkness reside? Can you take them to their places? Do you know the paths to their dwellings? Surely you know, for you were already born! You have lived so many years! "Have you entered the storehouses of the snow or seen the storehouses of the hail, which I reserve for times of trouble, for days of war and battle? What is the way to the place where the lightning is dispersed, or the place where the east winds are scattered over the earth? Who cuts a channel for the torrents of rain, and a path for the thunderstorm, to water a land where no man lives, a desert with no one in it, to satisfy a desolate wasteland and make it sprout with grass? Does the rain have a father? Who fathers the drops of dew? From whose womb comes the ice? Who gives birth to the frost from the heavens when the waters become hard as stone, when the surface of the deep is frozen? "Can you bind the beautiful Pleiades? Can you loose the cords of Orion? Can you bring forth the constellations in their seasons or lead out the Bear with its cubs? Do you know the laws of the heavens? Can you set up God's dominion over the earth? "Can you raise your voice to the clouds and cover yourself with a flood of water? Do you send the lightning bolts on their way? Do they report to you, 'Here we are'? Who endowed the heart with wisdom or gave understanding to the mind? Who has the wisdom to count the clouds? Who can tip over the water jars of the heavens when the dust becomes hard and the clods of earth stick together? "Do you hunt the prey for the lioness and satisfy the hunger of the lions when they crouch in their dens or lie in wait in a thicket? Who provides food for the raven when its young cry out to God and wander about for lack of food? (Job 38:1–41 NIV)

God Is Faithful

In chapter 3, we discussed God's faithfulness. We know we can put our trust in him because he is faithful. Throughout the Holy Scriptures, we see many promises and covenants God made with his people. Because God is faithful, he keeps his promises even when his people may prove to be unfaithful.

> The Lord did not set his heart on you and choose you because you were more numerous than other nations, for you were the smallest of all nations! Rather, it was simply that the Lord loves you, and he was keeping the oath he had sworn to your ancestors. That is why the Lord rescued you with such a strong hand from your slavery and from the oppressive hand of Pharaoh, king of Egypt. Understand, therefore, that the Lord your God is indeed God. He is the faithful God who keeps his covenant for a thousand generations and lavishes his unfailing love on those who love him and obey his commands. But he does not hesitate to punish and destroy those who reject him.

> Therefore, you must obey all these commands, decrees, and regulations I am giving you today. (Deuteronomy 7:7–11 NLT)

Through the Word of God, we learn that he is unchanging and promises to never leave us or forsake us. God walked with ancient Israel for thousands of years, and at the appointed time, he wrapped himself in flesh and came to earth (see John 1:14). When the Word became flesh (Jesus) and dwelled among us, he continued demonstrating his faithfulness to mankind through his powerful ministry by preaching the gospel to the poor, healing the brokenhearted, raising the dead, opening the eyes of the blind, setting captives free, etc. (see Luke 4:18–19). As the time neared for Jesus to go back to the Father, he assured God's people that they would not be left alone. He prayed God would send back his Holy Spirit to be with his people. God's faithfulness is as strong today as it was from the beginning. He has not left us to walk out this journey alone. We have his Holy Spirit, who is our spirit of truth, Comforter, witness, Guide, teacher, and so much more.

God Is Personal

It is important for us to understand the truth about God's character. When we learn of God, we can confidently put trust in him and therefore submit to his will. Another one of the many characteristics of God is that he is a personal Lord and Savior. He personally touches each of our lives, and as our personal Shepherd, he seeks to lead us through every path of our lives. Who is God to you personally?

Is He Your Provider?

In the Lord's Prayer (see Matthew 6:9–13), when Jesus prays, "Give us this day our daily bread," he is confessing that God is our provider. Does he not provide food on your table and clothing on your back and the backs of your children? Does he not provide your shelter? Even for the homeless, he provides food and shelter. "And my God will supply all your needs according to His riches in glory in Christ Jesus" (Philippians 4:19 NASB). Consider the following passage:

> Therefore I tell you, do not worry about your life, what you will eat or drink; or about your body, what you will wear. Is not life more important than food, and the body more important than clothes? Look at the birds of the air; they do not sow or reap or store away in barns, and yet your heavenly Father feeds them. Are you not much more valuable than they? Who of you by worrying add a single hour to his life? "And why do you worry about clothes? See how the lilies of the field grow. They do not labor or spin. Yet I tell you that not even Solomon in all his splendor was dressed like one of these. If that is how God clothes the grass of the field, which is here today and tomorrow is thrown into the fire, will he not much more clothe you, O you of little faith? (Matthew 6:25–30 NIV)

Is he your way maker?

Have you ever been in a situation where your back was up against the wall and there seemed to be no way out? Even lying, cheating, and stealing could not deliver you, but God did. Oh yes, God will make a way when there is no other way. When God delivered the children of Israel out of slavery in Egypt, they found themselves being fiercely pursued by the Egyptians (their enemies). When they came to the Red Sea and saw that mountains surrounded them on the sides, they knew they had nowhere else to escape; however, by the favor and grace of their almighty, all-powerful God, he parted the Red Sea, and the children of Israel (God's people) walked on dry ground through the sea to the other side. God will do things for his people that he will not do for those who are not his. There is no situation or circumstance too hard for our great God.

> As Pharaoh approached, the people of Israel looked up and panicked when they saw the Egyptians overtaking them. They cried out to the Lord, and they said to Moses, "Why did you bring us out here to die in the wilderness? Weren't there enough graves for us in Egypt? What have you done to us? Why did you make us leave Egypt? Didn't we tell you this would happen while we were still in Egypt? We said, 'Leave us alone! Let us be slaves to the Egyptians. It's better to be a slave in Egypt than a corpse in the wilderness!'" But Moses told the people, "Don't be afraid. Just stand still and watch the Lord rescue you today. The Egyptians you see today will never be seen again. The Lord himself will fight for you. Just stay calm." Then the Lord said to Moses, "Why are you crying out to me? Tell the people to get moving! Pick up your staff and raise your hand over the sea. Divide the water so the Israelites can

walk through the middle of the sea on dry ground. And I will harden the hearts of the Egyptians, and they will charge in after the Israelites. My great glory will be displayed through Pharaoh and his troops, his chariots, and his charioteers. When my glory is displayed through them, all Egypt will see my glory and know that I am the Lord!" Then the angel of God, who had been leading the people of Israel, moved to the rear of the camp. The pillar of cloud also moved from the front and stood behind them. The cloud settled between the Egyptian and Israelite camps. As darkness fell, the cloud turned to fire, lighting up the night. But the Egyptians and Israelites did not approach each other all night. Then Moses raised his hand over the sea, and the Lord opened up a path through the water with a strong east wind. The wind blew all that night, turning the seabed into dry land. So the people of Israel walked through the middle of the sea on dry ground, with walls of water on each side! Then the Egyptians—all of Pharaoh's horses, chariots, and charioteers—chased them into the middle of the sea. But just before dawn the Lord looked down on the Egyptian army from the pillar of fire and cloud, and he threw their forces into total confusion. He twisted their chariot wheels, making their chariots difficult to drive. "Let's get out of here—away from these Israelites!" the Egyptians shouted. "The Lord is fighting for them against Egypt!" When all the Israelites had reached the other side, the Lord said to Moses, "Raise your hand over the sea again. Then the waters will rush back and cover the Egyptians and their chariots and charioteers." So as the sun began to rise, Moses raised his hand over the sea, and the water rushed back into its usual place. The Egyptians tried to escape, but the Lord swept them into the sea. Then the waters returned and covered all the chariots and charioteers—the entire army of Pharaoh. Of all the Egyptians who had chased the Israelites into the sea, not a single one survived. (Exodus 14:10–28 NLT)

Is he your healer?

At some point in each of our lives, we have or will be faced with an illness. And although we have been blessed with many discoveries through science for curing sickness and diseases, the discoveries could not have been possible without our Creator and the maker of all things, God. The Creator of man is the one who gives man all revelation and knowledge and the capacity to contain such revelation and knowledge. But God, our Creator, can go much further than mere scientific discoveries for curing sicknesses and diseases. He is the cure. He is our healer, and he is in the business of working miracles. Whether he speaks a word so that we are healed or he gives his healing solution to mankind, God is our healer. God loves and cares for mankind, and there is no sickness, no disease, and no illness beyond his healing power. By the stripes of Jesus Christ, we are healed. We just need to believe in his healing power.

On the other side of the lake the crowds welcomed Jesus, because they had been waiting for him. Then a man named Jairus, a leader of the local synagogue, came and fell at Jesus's feet, pleading with him to come home with him. His only daughter, who was about twelve years old, was dying. As Jesus went with him, he was surrounded by the crowds. A woman in the crowd had suffered for twelve years with constant bleeding, and she could find no cure. Coming up behind Jesus, she touched the fringe of his robe. Immediately, the bleeding stopped. "Who touched me?" Jesus asked. Everyone denied it, and Peter said, "Master, this whole crowd is pressing up against you." But Jesus said, "Someone deliberately touched me, for I felt healing power go out from me." When the woman realized that she could not stay hidden, she began to tremble and fell to her knees in front of him. The whole crowd heard her explain why she had touched him and that she had been immediately healed. "Daughter," he said to her, "your faith has made you well. Go in peace." While he was still speaking to her, a messenger arrived from the home of Jairus, the leader of the synagogue. He told him, "Your daughter is dead. There's no use troubling the Teacher now." But when Jesus heard what had happened, he said to Jairus, "Don't be afraid. Just have faith, and she will be healed." When they arrived at the house, Jesus wouldn't let anyone go in with him except Peter, John, James, and the little girl's father and mother. The house was filled with people weeping and wailing, but he said, "Stop the weeping! She isn't dead; she's only asleep." But the crowd laughed at him because they all knew she had died. Then Jesus took her by the hand and said in a loud voice, "My child, get up!" And at that moment her life returned, and she immediately stood up! Then Jesus told them to give her something to eat. Her parents were overwhelmed, but Jesus insisted that they not tell anyone what had happened. (Luke 8:40–56 NLT)

Is he your peace?

When all turmoil is breaking loose and our lives seem to be spiraling out of control, there is always a place to go for peace. Several years ago I was driving on the freeway on my way to work. As I traveled through a construction zone, there was an area where the shoulder of the highway ended, and barriers had been placed on the line of the shoulder. Much to my surprise, I got too close, and my tire clipped the barrier, sending my SUV into the air. It landed on its side, slid for about a hundred feet on the pavement, and came to a rest on the shoulder of the highway. This accident occurred in the morning rush-hour traffic, and miraculously no other cars were involved. I escaped the tragic incident without injury, but my inner self was completely shaken. I couldn't understand what was going on and why this had happened. When I returned home later that morning, I knew I needed to find peace. So I opened my Bible and found a section with Scriptures that covered specific topics. I flipped through the pages and found the topic of peace, and there it was. My spirit was pointing right to the

Word (medicine) I needed, specifically Psalm 91. I began to read that Scripture, and almost immediately I felt peace come in and fill my body. It was as if I had just drunk the antidote for my torment, fear, and sufferings. I found so much peace in this word that I fell right to sleep.

> He who dwells in the secret place of the Most
> High
> Shall abide under the shadow of the Almighty.
> I will say of the Lord, "He is my refuge and my
> fortress;
> My God, in Him I will trust."
> Surely He shall deliver you from the snare of the
> fowler
> And from the perilous pestilence.
> He shall cover you with His feathers,
> And under His wings you shall take refuge;
> His truth shall be your shield and buckler.
> You shall not be afraid of the terror by night,
> Nor of the arrow that flies by day,
> Nor of the pestilence that walks in darkness,
> Nor of the destruction that lays waste at noonday.
> A thousand may fall at your side,
> And ten thousand at your right hand;
> But it shall not come near you.
> Only with your eyes shall you look,
> And see the reward of the wicked.
> Because you have made the Lord, who is my
> refuge,
> Even the Most High, your dwelling place,
> No evil shall befall you,

Nor shall any plague come near your dwelling;
For He shall give His angels charge over you,
To keep you in all your ways.
In their hands they shall bear you up,
Lest you dash your foot against a stone.
You shall tread upon the lion and the cobra,
The young lion and the serpent you shall trample
underfoot.
"Because he has set his love upon Me, therefore I
will deliver him;
I will set him on high, because he has known My
name.
He shall call upon Me, and I will answer him;
I will be with him in trouble;
I will deliver him and honor him.
With long life I will satisfy him,
And show him My salvation."
(Psalm 91 NKJV)

Is he your Alpha and Omega (your beginning and your end)?
God is our internal GPS. He knows where we came from, he knows our current location in life, and he knows where we are going. The all-knowing and all-powerful God possess the complete set of plans and knows the exact purpose for each of our lives (see Jeremiah 29:11). He made all the delicate, inner parts of our bodies and knit us together in our mother's wombs (see Psalm 139:13 NLT). Not only has he created and purposed each of us, but he has also provided our roadmap to success and prosperity—the map that will lead us right into our purpose and destiny. It does not get any better than this. Solomon advised us in Ecclesiastes that unless we take God's way (our source from

the beginning to the end), everything that we ever seek after and accomplish in life is in meaningless. God knows the plan for each of our lives from beginning to end. The Lord spoke to Jeremiah and said, "I knew you before I formed you in your mother's womb. Before you were born I set you apart and appointed you as my prophet to the nations" (Jeremiah 1:5 NLT).

Has he become your everything?

In our intimate relationship with God, we must allow him to become our everything, which will produce hearts willing to completely submit to his perfect will for our lives. Perhaps the most extreme example of submission to God's perfect will was demonstrated through our Lord and Savior, Jesus Christ. After the Passover meal and as the time drew near for Jesus to sacrifice his life for the sins of the world, he went out to the Garden of Gethsemane and prayed. He prayed with great anguish, asking God to take the assignment from him; but that if it be not his will, then nevertheless, not my will, but God's will be done. He was beaten, thronged, and forced to bear his own cross, but nevertheless, God's will was done. He was nailed on the cross through his hands and his feet, pierced in his side, and crowned with a crown of thorns, but nevertheless, God's will was done. As the Son of God, knowing he was about to experience a period of spiritual separation from God, he could have aborted the assignment and came down from the cross, but instead he obeyed and submitted to the will of God and gave his last breath.

> Then the governor's soldiers took Jesus into the Praetorium and gathered the whole company of soldiers around him. They stripped him and put a scarlet robe on him, and then twisted together a

crown of thorns and set it on his head. They put a staff in his right hand and knelt in front of him and mocked him. "Hail, king of the Jews!" they said. They spit on him, and took the staff and struck him on the head again and again. After they had mocked him, they took off the robe and put his own clothes on him. Then they led him away to crucify him. As they were going out, they met a man from Cyrene, named Simon, and they forced him to carry the cross. They came to a place called Golgotha (which means "the place of the skull"). There they offered Jesus wine to drink, mixed with gall; but after tasting it, he refused to drink it. When they had crucified him, they divided up his clothes by casting lots. And sitting down, they kept watch over him there. Above his head they placed the written charge against him: THIS IS JESUS, THE KING OF THE JEWS. Two robbers were crucified with him, one on his right and one on his left. Those who passed by hurled insults at him, shaking their heads and saying, "You who are going to destroy the temple and build it in three days, save yourself! Come down from the cross, if you are the Son of God!" In the same way the chief priests, the teachers of the law and the elders mocked him. "He saved others," they said, "but he can't save himself! He's the king of Israel! Let him come down now from the cross, and we will believe in him. He trusts in God. Let God rescue him now if he wants him, for he said, 'I am the

Son of God.'" In the same way the robbers who were crucified with him also heaped insults on him. From the sixth hour until the ninth hour darkness came over all the land. About the ninth hour Jesus cried out in a loud voice, "Eloi, Eloi, lama sabachthani?"–which means, "My God, my God, why have you forsaken me?" When some of those standing there heard this, they said, "He's calling Elijah." Immediately one of them ran and got a sponge. He filled it with wine vinegar, put it on a stick, and offered it to Jesus to drink. The rest said, "Now leave him alone. Let's see if Elijah comes to save him." And when Jesus had cried out again in a loud voice, he gave up his spirit. At that moment the curtain of the temple was torn in two from top to bottom. The earth shook and the rocks split. The tombs broke open and the bodies of many holy people who had died were raised to life. They came out of the tombs, and after Jesus' resurrection they went into the holy city and appeared to many people. When the centurion and those with him who were guarding Jesus saw the earthquake and all that had happened, they were terrified, and exclaimed, "Surely he was the Son of God!" (Matthew 27:27–54 NIV)

CHAPTER 6

A Pure Heart

Previously, we discussed the importance of putting all of our trust in God. When we trust God in every aspect of our lives, we can submit to following his divine leadership. Do you trust God? You may say, "Oh yes, I trust God. He is and has been my everything." Trust in God is a key spiritual value we must obtain and maintain in an intimate relationship with God. If you confess that you trust God, you must then ask, "Can God trust me? Can I be faithful to God as he is to me?" As you walk in a personal and intimate relationship with Him, are your motives pure? Can he trust you to yield your self-will to him? Can he trust you to obey his commands and pursue the assignment or purpose he has for you? Can he trust you to sow the seeds he has given you to sow—seeds of kindness, time and patience with others, wisdom, knowledge, information, or even monetary seeds. Can he trust you with the souls of the brokenhearted? Can he trust you to bring the truth of his Word to set captives free? Can he trust you to genuinely love others?

The psalmist David, a trusted servant of the Lord, says, "Who may ascend into the hill of the Lord? Or who may stand in His holy place? He who has clean hands and a pure heart, Who has not lifted up his soul to an idol, Nor sworn deceitfully. He shall receive blessing from the Lord, And righteousness from the God of his salvation" (Psalm 24:3–5 NKJV). God can trust those servants with clean hands and pure hearts with his work in the earth realm. God honors his faithful servants who remain blameless and who walk holy before him.

> When Herod was king of Judea, there was a Jewish priest named Zechariah. He was a member of the priestly order of Abijah, and his wife, Elizabeth, was also from the priestly line of Aaron. Zechariah and Elizabeth were righteous in God's eyes, careful to obey all of the Lord's commandments and regulations. They had no children because Elizabeth was unable to conceive, and they were both very old. One day Zechariah was serving God in the Temple, for his order was on duty that week. As was the custom of the priests, he was chosen by lot to enter the sanctuary of the Lord and burn incense. While the incense was being burned, a great crowd stood outside, praying. While Zechariah was in the sanctuary, an angel of the Lord appeared to him, standing to the right of the incense altar. Zechariah was shaken and overwhelmed with fear when he saw him. But the angel said, "Don't be afraid, Zechariah! God has heard your prayer. Your wife, Elizabeth, will give you a son, and you are to name him John. You will have great joy and gladness, and many will rejoice at his birth, for he will be great in the

eyes of the Lord. He must never touch wine or other alcoholic drinks. He will be filled with the Holy Spirit, even before his birth. And he will turn many Israelites to the Lord their God. He will be a man with the spirit and power of Elijah. He will prepare the people for the coming of the Lord. He will turn the hearts of the fathers to their children, and he will cause those who are rebellious to accept the wisdom of the godly." Zechariah said to the angel, "How can I be sure this will happen? I'm an old man now, and my wife is also well along in years." Then the angel said, "I am Gabriel! I stand in the very presence of God. It was he who sent me to bring you this good news! But now, since you didn't believe what I said, you will be silent and unable to speak until the child is born. For my words will certainly be fulfilled at the proper time." Meanwhile, the people were waiting for Zechariah to come out of the sanctuary, wondering why he was taking so long. When he finally did come out, he couldn't speak to them. Then they realized from his gestures and his silence that he must have seen a vision in the sanctuary. When Zechariah's week of service in the Temple was over, he returned home. Soon afterward his wife, Elizabeth, became pregnant and went into seclusion for five months. "How kind the Lord is!" she exclaimed. "He has taken away my disgrace of having no children." (Luke 1:5–25 NLT)

Zechariah and Elizabeth were faithful servants whose hearts were pure, and they walked holy before the Lord, their God. They had no children because Elizabeth was barren; however, they did not let that issue hinder them from their covenant relationship with God. In those days, having children symbolized a blessed life while not having children was looked upon as a curse. Despite their disgraceful circumstance of being childless, they continued as faithful and obedient servants who worshipped the Lord wholeheartedly.

One day as Zechariah prayed in the presence of God, God heard his prayer and answered him with some mind-blowing news. He and his wife were going to have a son, and his name would be John. When God brings us into his presence, we never leave the same way we entered. We conceive, and come out pregnant with that which the Lord has promised. Zechariah was in complete amazement over the news he had just heard from the Lord. He and his wife were fairly old and well past the age for bearing children, so in his attempt to understand this fact from a human perspective, Zechariah doubted God's promise. Because he doubted God's message, which was spoken by the angel (Gabriel), God caused a spirit of dumbness to come upon him, making him unable to speak. But in his very own order and timing, God delivered on his promise to Zechariah and Elizabeth. They conceived and gave birth to a son. The couple was foretold by the angel Gabriel that their son was no ordinary person but that he was chosen to prepare the way for the coming Messiah. What a difference a pure heart makes! Just when it seems you may be forgotten, God hears your call and your cry. He can trust those who have pure hearts with his most precious and critical work in the earth realm. Although Zechariah went through a stormy season of doubt, he and his wife's hearts remained pure in the eyes of God, and God remained faithful and merciful to them, his servants. He could trust Zechariah and Elizabeth with this divine assignment to bring forth and rear up one of God's most extraordinary servants, John the Baptist.

Each and every one of us are born with a God-given purpose. Our true purpose in the earth is all for the glory of God. In your relationship with God, not only are you to trust him wholeheartedly, but God must also be able to trust you to learn of him and become his faithful servant so that he can trust you with his promised assignment for your life. Can God trust you to be dedicated and devoted without motives for self-gain?

A Pure Heart

What is a pure heart? As we can see from Zechariah and Elizabeth, God deeply honors those whose hearts are pure. Let us look deeper into the lifestyle of this couple to hopefully gain insight into how we, too, can be trusted by the almighty God with his promise(s). They both came from a priestly lineage, which gave them the advantage of learning godly principles at an early age. From watching our parents and family, we, too, learn most of their behaviors (whether good or evil) and mimic them in our adulthood. Clearly both Zechariah and Elizabeth learned to worship God wholeheartedly. They trusted God and therefore gave themselves over to his service and will. As faithful followers of God's law, they were more than willing to serve others and serve on the behalf of others. Their service to God was not selfishly motivated but was solely and unselfishly done out of obedience to the will of God. When our hearts are pure, we unselfishly operate and conduct our affairs according to the heart of God. A pure heart comes from the heart of God. A pure heart is a heart that is right with God. Anyone functioning out of the heart of God serves unselfishly and gives of him or herself for the health, welfare, and betterment of humanity.

A pure heart is a very important character value in the eyes of God. It is a must-have credential for God to trust us with his most precious possessions and critical work in the earth realm. Although a pure heart is its own pillar or value, it is also the heartbeat and support of the other six pillars in this book. For example, if a man has trust (in God) and is obedient to God's will, but his heart is not pure; then he is not reflecting the fullness of trust or obedience unto God. God is looking for us to give him our all. In order for our character values of trust, obedience, humility, patience, love, and submission to manifest to their fullest capacity in our lives, a pure heart must be added to give each pillar its full support. As you can see, a pure heart completes the package. A pure heart is to the other six pillars as rebar is to the pillars that support a bridge. What I am saying here is that without a pure heart, it is impossible to fully live a virtuous lifestyle for God. As a man honors his virtuous wife, so does God honor his virtuous children, servants, and family.

What Happens If Our Hearts Are Not Pure?

Saul was thirty years old when he became king, and he reigned for forty-two years. Saul selected 3,000 special troops from the army of Israel and sent the rest of the men home. He took 2,000 of the chosen men with him to Micmash and the hill country of Bethel. The other 1,000 went with Saul's son Jonathan to Gibeah in the land of Benjamin. Soon after this, Jonathan attacked and defeated the garrison of Philistines at Geba. The news spread quickly among the Philistines. So Saul blew the ram's horn throughout the land, saying, "Hebrews, hear this! Rise up in revolt!" All Israel heard the news that Saul had destroyed the Philistine garrison at Geba and that the Philistines now hated the Israelites more than ever. So the entire Israelite army was summoned to join Saul at Gilgal. The Philistines mustered a mighty army of 3,000 chariots, 6,000 charioteers, and as many warriors as the grains of sand on the seashore! They camped at Micmash east of Beth- aven. The men of Israel saw what a tight spot they were in; and because they were hard pressed by the enemy, they tried to hide in caves, thickets, rocks, holes, and cisterns. Some of them crossed the Jordan River and escaped into the land of Gad and Gilead. Meanwhile, Saul stayed at Gilgal, and his men were trembling with fear. Saul waited there seven days for Samuel, as Samuel had instructed him earlier, but Samuel still didn't come. Saul realized that his troops were rapidly slipping away. So he demanded, "Bring me the burnt offering and the peace offerings!" And Saul sacrificed the burnt offering himself. Just as Saul was finishing with the burnt offering, Samuel arrived. Saul went out to meet and welcome him, but Samuel said, "What is this you have done?"

Saul replied, "I saw my men scattering from me, and you didn't arrive when you said you would, and the Philistines are at Micmash ready for battle. So I said, 'The Philistines are ready to march against us at Gilgal, and I haven't even asked for the Lord's help!' So I felt compelled to offer the burnt offering myself before you came." "How foolish!" Samuel exclaimed. "You have not kept the command the Lord your God gave you. Had you kept it, the Lord would have established your kingdom over Israel forever. But now your kingdom must end, for the Lord has sought out a man after his own heart. The Lord has already appointed him to be the leader of his people, because you have not kept the Lord's command." (1 Samuel 13:1–14 NLT)

Prior to Saul's reign as king over Israel, God appointed representatives (judges) to lead his people while he himself reigned as their true leader (King). The children of Israel grew tired of this system of government, and the judges were more and more turning away from following the commands and ways of God. Even Samuel's sons served as judges but were corrupt. Where there is corruption, there's deterioration and destruction. Corruption changes the pure to impure. Corruption stems from the impure (unclean) motives of a person or a group of people seeking self-gain. After many years of corruption within the judges and deterioration in many areas within the nation, including a lack of unity among the tribes, and a weakened and disorganized army, the people began to look for change in their governmental system, Israel began to recognize they did not have a king to lead them like the multitudes of nations around them, so they demanded the prophet Samuel to ask God for a king to rule over them. This was not God's will for his people, but he gave them exactly what they asked for, a king. God chose Saul to reign as Israel's first king. Samuel obeyed God's command and anointed Saul as king of Israel.

During his reign as king, Saul struggled with living the spiritual values God requires. He was insecure within himself, and ignorant to God's awesome power and glory as his resource for leading; therefore, Saul trusted in his own power and might and not in the Lord. Saul was also a very proud and selfish person who found it difficult to totally and consistently submit to the will of God. One of his biggest character flaws was disobedience. Instead of obedience to God, Saul chose his own way of leading God's people, treating them and speaking to them however he wished. This is precisely an issue that Samuel warned the people against in their want for a king to reign instead of keeping God as their king. Israel's own problem was that the people lacked obedience. They lacked pure wholehearted worship unto God, and therefore, they sought after their own way of living—no longer living for God but living according to their own rules and laws. When we move from under God's leadership and seek after our own way of life, God does not force us to remain in fellowship with him.

With their new king in place, the people began to follow his commands. Because of Saul's ignorance to the knowledge and power of God, he was unable to tap into the awesome leadership of God for leading the nation victoriously. Through the prophet Samuel, God instructed Saul in various battles. Although Saul and his Israelite army defeated their enemies, Saul had difficulty following and obeying the commands and timing of God. Saul's proud and selfish motives stood between him and God, causing God's people to suffer needlessly. Because of Saul's many acts of disobedience, many of which were caused by his proud and selfish motives, God could no longer trust Saul to lead his people (Israel). God removed the throne from Saul and sought for himself a man after his own heart, a man with a pure heart and pure motives to lead the nation of Israel.

A Man with a Pure Heart

David, known to God as "a man after Gods own heart" (see previous Scripture text), was the first king to be truly appointed from the heart of God to lead his people, Israel. David was an obedient servant and warrior whose heart was right in the eyes of God. Only God can read the motives of our hearts, and David's heart was found by God to be pure.

This may be a good time for us to reflect on our own hearts to determine our own motives. We can be like David and pray the following: "Search me, O God, and know my heart; test me and know my anxious thoughts. Point out anything in me that offends you, and lead me along the path of everlasting life" (Psalm 139:23-24 NLT). Are you allowing God to be your King and his Spirit to guide you in making all decisions? David not only had a heart for God, but he also operated out of the heart of God. He sought wholeheartedly to live for God. He worshipped God wholeheartedly through the Law, through prayer, and through praise and worship. He sought the Lord for matters concerning his leadership role as well as the welfare of

God's people. During his reign as king, David sought the Lord concerning every decision, including whether or not to enter into battle with their enemies. Even through most of David's reign over all of Israel (Israel and Judah), the Philistines continued as Israel's chief and most powerful enemy. The Scripture to follow gives us insight on how much David relied on God's instructions and commands for leading his nation through multitudes of battles victoriously. Relying on God's leadership unleashes the power of his Holy Spirit to work on our behalf and see us through our battles victoriously.

When the Philistines heard that David had been anointed king of Israel, they mobilized all their forces to capture him. But David was told they were coming, so he went into the stronghold. The Philistines arrived and spread out across the valley of Rephaim. So David asked the Lord, "Should I go out to fight the Philistines? Will you hand them over to me?" The Lord replied to David, "Yes, go ahead. I will certainly hand them over to you." So David went to Baal-perazim and defeated the Philistines there. "The Lord did it!" David exclaimed. "He burst through my enemies like a raging flood!" So he named that place Baal-perazim (which means "the Lord who bursts through"). The Philistines had abandoned their idols there, so David and his men confiscated them. But after a while the Philistines returned and again spread out across the valley of Rephaim. And again David asked the Lord what to do. "Do not attack them straight on," the Lord replied.

"Instead, circle around behind and attack them near the poplar trees. When you hear a sound like marching feet in the tops of the poplar trees, be on the alert! That will be the signal that the Lord is moving ahead of you to strike down the Philistine army." So David did what the Lord commanded, and he struck down the Philistines all the way from Gibeon to Gezer. (2 Samuel 5:17–25 NLT)

David victoriously led God's people because he chose God as his leader and King. He carefully followed God's instructions for the battle and gave God the glory for the victories. This life principle is still in full force and effect today. When we choose God as our leader and King, we will be victorious in everything we set our hands to, and we must give him the glory at all times for the victory. It is not by our own might or by our own power but by the Spirit of the Lord (see Zechariah 4:6) that we shall walk in and live victorious lives.

Through faith David came to know God and trusted in him with all his heart. David was never too proud to heed God's Word, commands, and/or instructions, which demonstrated his heart pure in the eyes of God.

I know most of you reading this book may be saying to yourselves, "Yeah, but David committed adultery, killed, stole, lied, and lusted after a man's wife;" and I say, "Yes, you are absolutely right!" David had his own share of sins and was not always perfect in character and/or judgment concerning his personal life.

In the spring, at the time when kings go off to war, David sent Joab out with the king's men and the whole Israelite army. They destroyed the Ammonites and besieged Rabbah. But David remained in Jerusalem. One evening David got up from his bed and walked around on the roof of the palace. From the roof he saw a woman bathing. The woman was very beautiful, and David sent someone to find out about her. The man said, "Isn't this Bathsheba, the daughter of Eliam and the wife of Uriah the Hittite?" Then David sent messengers to get her. She came to him, and he slept with her. (She had purified herself from her uncleanness.) Then she went back home. The woman conceived and sent word to David, saying, "I am pregnant." So David sent this word to Joab: "Send me Uriah the Hittite." And Joab sent him to David. When Uriah came to him, David asked him how Joab was, how the soldiers were and how the war was going. Then David said to Uriah, "Go down to your house and wash your feet." So Uriah left the palace, and a gift from the king was sent after him. But Uriah slept at the entrance to the palace with all his master's servants and did not go down to his house. When David was told, "Uriah did not go home," he asked him, "Haven't you just come from a distance? Why didn't you go home?" Uriah said to David, "The ark and Israel and Judah are staying in tents, and my master Joab and my lord's men are camped in the open fields.

How could I go to my house to eat and drink and lie with my wife? As surely as you live, I will not do such a thing!" Then David said to him, "Stay here one more day, and tomorrow I will send you back." So Uriah remained in Jerusalem that day and the next. At David's invitation, he ate and drank with him, and David made him drunk. But in the evening Uriah went out to sleep on his mat among his master's servants; he did not go home. In the morning David wrote a letter to Joab and sent it with Uriah. In it he wrote, "Put Uriah in the front line where the fighting is fiercest. Then withdraw from him so he will be struck down and die." So while Joab had the city under siege, he put Uriah at a place where he knew the strongest defenders were. When the men of the city came out and fought against Joab, some of the men in David's army fell; moreover, Uriah the Hittite died. Joab sent David a full account of the battle. He instructed the messenger: "When you have finished giving the king this account of the battle, the king's anger may flare up, and he may ask you, 'Why did you get so close to the city to fight? Didn't you know they would shoot arrows from the wall? Who killed Abimelek son of Jerub-Besheth? Didn't a woman throw an upper millstone on him from the wall, so that he died in Thebez? Why did you get so close to the wall?' If he asks you this, then say to him, 'Also, your servant Uriah the Hittite is dead.'" The messenger set out, and when he arrived he told

David everything Joab had sent him to say. The messenger said to David, "The men overpowered us and came out against us in the open, but we drove them back to the entrance to the city gate. Then the archers shot arrows at your servants from the wall, and some of the king's men died. Moreover, your servant Uriah the Hittite is dead." David told the messenger, "Say this to Joab: 'Don't let this upset you; the sword devours one as well as another. Press the attack against the city and destroy it.' Say this to encourage Joab." When Uriah's wife heard that her husband was dead, she mourned for him. After the time of mourning was over, David had her brought to his house, and she became his wife and bore him a son. But the thing David had done displeased the Lord. (2 Samuel 11:1–27 NIV)

Just this one situation of folly in David's life caused him to commit a multitude of sins. One sin brought on another sin. For starters, David, according to his own will, chose to stay at his palace and not go to war with his men, putting himself in the wrong place at the wrong time. As he walked along the roof of his palace, he saw a beautiful woman taking a shower. At that moment lust entered his heart, and temptation was right before his eyes. Instead of asking God to help him overcome the temptation, he decided to dabble around and find out who this beautiful woman was. Once we begin to entertain temptation, especially in the areas where we are weak, it seems like the ball keeps rolling until we end up yielding to the temptation. We must stop temptation in its tracks by praying and seeking

God for help and then trusting that he will deliver us and see us through. Prayerfully you will also find an understanding confidant with whom you can discuss your weakness. In this case, David yielded to temptation and slept with Bathsheba, Uriah's wife. After he committed adultery, David sought to cover up his sin, which resulted in him killing Uriah and many others losing their lives. The more he sinned, the more insensitive to sin he became. David's sins affected not only his own life but the lives of countless others, including his own household and loved ones. At this point David's sinful lifestyle was beginning to look like Saul's. He used his kingship position to get what he wanted, and many innocent people were being hurt or killed.

God, who is a *righteous* and *just* God, did not allow David to go unpunished for his sins. God sent one of his prophets named Nathan to inform David that he was aware of his sins and that David must suffer the consequences of the sins he has committed. God promised David that he would not kill him; however, the Lord did say that the child he had conceived with Bathsheba, another man's wife, would surely die.

When David finally came to his senses, realizing the error of his sinful ways, he fell to his knees and earnestly sought the Lord for forgiveness. David asked God to create in him a clean heart and renew a right spirit within him (see Psalm 51:10). His prayer to God came from a heart of repentance, one of complete sorrow for his sins against God. One of the splendors of God's grace is forgiveness of sins. God makes forgiveness available to us all when we sin. You, too, can drop to your knees and with a heart of repentance, ask God's forgiveness of your sins. Even now he is listening. God forgave David of his sins, and David put the sins of his past behind and began a renewed life and relationship with God.

The Pure v. Impure Heart

Here we have two men, Saul and David, who were both kings and both sinned in the eyes of God. One man's heart was found to be impure, and he could not be trusted by God to lead; however, the other man was found to have a pure heart, and he could be trusted by God to lead. If both men were sinners, then what was it about their hearts that made one impure and one pure? Again, only God can read the hearts of man. The impure heart is one that has no regard for God's moral and spiritual principles. An impure heart also does not confess sins and earnestly seek God's forgiveness of those sins. On the other hand, one with a pure heart does not allow the guilt of sin to remain but instead seeks to come into right standing with God, taking heed and supporting God's moral principles. A pure heart confesses his or her sins and wholeheartedly seeks God to forgive those sins.

In 2 Chronicles 7:14 (NIV), God responds to Solomon's prayer and says, "If my people, who are called by my name, will humble themselves and pray and seek my face and turn from their wicked ways, then will I hear from heaven and will forgive their sin and will heal their land."

God promises forgiveness to all those who come to him humbled and with a heart of repentance. In Psalm 32, David expressed the great joy he felt when God forgave him of his sins.

Oh, what joy for those
whose disobedience is forgiven,
whose sin is put out of sight!
Yes, what joy for those
whose record the Lord has cleared of guilt,
whose lives are lived in complete honesty!
When I refused to confess my sin,
my body wasted away,
and I groaned all day long.
Day and night your hand of discipline was heavy
on me.
My strength evaporated like water in the summer
heat. Interlude
Finally, I confessed all my sins to you
and stopped trying to hide my guilt.
I said to myself, "I will confess my rebellion to
the Lord."
And you forgave me! All my guilt is gone. Interlude
Therefore, let all the godly pray to you while there
is still time,
that they may not drown in the floodwaters of
judgment.
For you are my hiding place;
you protect me from trouble.
You surround me with songs of victory. Interlude
The Lord says, "I will guide you along the best
pathway for your life.

I will advise you and watch over you.
Do not be like a senseless horse or mule
that needs a bit and bridle to keep it under
control."
Many sorrows come to the wicked,
but unfailing love surrounds those who trust the
Lord.
So rejoice in the Lord and be glad, all you who
obey him!
Shout for joy, all you whose hearts are pure!
(Psalm 32:1–11 NLT)

CHAPTER 7

Obedience

Through the course of writing this book, I can't tell you the countless times that the Holy Spirit awakened me in the early morning hours to write. Out of a heart (my heart) that seeks to please God and that puts more trust in God than the desire of my flesh, I would find the inner strength to obey his voice over my own will and desire to sleep. For many of us, one, two, and three o'clock in the morning are prime time for sleeping. We would rather drop back off to sleep than get up and write a book. Our spirit within may be willing, but our flesh is weak. Our flesh fights to remain in a place of comfort—in this case, that warm and cozy bed. So what should we do? Should we obey the voice of the Spirit (the Holy Spirit), or should we obey the will of our flesh? God has given all of humanity the free will to choose who they will obey.

Our entire lives are filled with choices. Every day we must morally choose between right and wrong, good and bad, obedience and disobedience, beautiful and ugly, staying or going, and the list goes on. Our choices will determine our destiny. Some choices lead us to life or death, blessings or curses. In the text to follow, we will find that obedience to God is the ultimate principle we must follow for prosperous and successful lives.

> If you fully obey the Lord your God and carefully follow all his commands I give you today, the Lord your God will set you high above all the nations on earth. All these blessings will come upon you and accompany you if you obey the Lord your God: You will be blessed in the city and blessed in the country. The fruit of your womb will be blessed, and the crops of your land and the young of your livestock—the calves of your herds and the lambs of your flocks. Your basket and your kneading trough will be blessed. You will be blessed when you come in and blessed when you go out. The Lord will grant that the enemies who rise up against you will be defeated before you. They will come at you from one direction but flee from you in seven. The Lord will send a blessing on your barns and on everything you put your hand to. The Lord your God will bless you in the land he is giving you. The Lord will establish you as his holy people, as he promised you on oath, if you keep the commands of the Lord your God and walk in his ways. Then all the peoples on earth will see that you are called by the name of the Lord, and they will fear you. The Lord will grant you abundant prosperity— in the fruit of your womb, the young of your livestock and the crops of your ground—in the land he swore to your forefathers to give you.

The Lord will open the heavens, the storehouse of his bounty, to send rain on your land in season and to bless all the work of your hands. You will lend to many nations but will borrow from none. The Lord will make you the head, not the tail. If you pay attention to the commands of the Lord your God that I give you this day and carefully follow them, you will always be at the top, never at the bottom. Do not turn aside from any of the commands I give you today, to the right or to the left, following other gods and serving them. (Deuteronomy 28:1–14 NIV)

Conversely, if we choose not to obey the voice of God and all that he commands of us, we will find our lives filled with much folly, lack, defeat, and failure.

However, if you do not obey the Lord your God and do not carefully follow all his commands and decrees I am giving you today, all these curses will come upon you and overtake you: You will be cursed in the city and cursed in the country. Your basket and your kneading trough will be cursed. The fruit of your womb will be cursed, and the crops of your land, and the calves of your herds and the lambs of your flocks. You will be cursed when you come in and cursed when you go out. The Lord will send on you curses, confusion and rebuke in everything you put your hand to, until you are destroyed and come to sudden ruin because of the evil you have done in forsaking him. The Lord will plague you with diseases until he has destroyed you from the land you are entering to possess. The Lord will strike you with wasting disease, with fever and inflammation, with scorching heat and drought, with blight and mildew, which will plague you until you perish. The sky over your head will be bronze, the ground beneath you iron. The Lord will turn the rain of your country into dust and powder; it will come down from the skies until you are destroyed. The Lord will cause you to be defeated before your enemies. You will come at them from one direction but flee from them in seven, and you will become a thing of horror to all the kingdoms on earth. Your carcasses will be food for all the birds of the air and the beasts of the earth, and there will be no one to frighten them away. The Lord will afflict you with the boils of Egypt and with tumors, festering sores and the itch, from which you cannot be cured. The Lord will afflict you with madness, blindness and confusion of mind. At midday you will grope about like a blind man in the dark. You will be unsuccessful in everything you do; day after day you will be oppressed and robbed, with no one to rescue you. You will be pledged to be married to a woman, but another will take her and ravish her. You will build a house, but you will not live in it. You will plant a vineyard, but you will not even begin to enjoy its fruit. Your ox will be slaughtered before your eyes, but you will eat none of it. Your donkey will be forcibly taken from you and will not be returned. Your sheep will be given to your enemies, and no one will rescue them. Your sons and daughters will be given to another nation, and you will wear out your eyes watching for them day after day, powerless to lift a hand. A people that you do not know will eat what your land and labor produce, and you will have nothing but cruel oppression all your days. The sights you see will drive you mad. The Lord will afflict your knees and legs with painful boils that cannot be cured, spreading from the soles of your feet to the top of your head. The Lord will drive you and the king you set over you to a nation unknown to you or your fathers. There you will worship other gods, gods of wood and stone. You will become a thing of horror and an object of scorn and ridicule to all the nations where the Lord will drive you. You will sow much seed in the field but you will harvest little, because locusts will devour it. You will plant vineyards and cultivate them but you will not drink the wine or gather the grapes, because worms will eat them. You will have olive trees throughout your country but you will not use the oil, because the olives will drop off. You will have sons and daughters but you will not keep them, because they will go into captivity. Swarms of locusts will take over all your trees and the crops of your land. The alien who lives among you will rise above you higher and higher, but you will sink lower and lower. He will lend to you, but you will not lend to him. He will be the head, but you will be the tail. All these curses will come upon you. They will pursue you and overtake you until you are destroyed, because you did not obey the Lord your God and observe the commands and decrees he gave you. They will be a sign and a wonder to you and your descendants forever. Because you did not serve the Lord your God joyfully and gladly in the time of prosperity, therefore in hunger and thirst, in nakedness and dire poverty, you will serve the enemies the Lord sends against you. He will put an iron yoke on your neck until he has destroyed you. The Lord will bring a nation against you from far away, from the ends of the earth, like an eagle swooping down, a nation whose language you will not understand, a fierce-looking nation without respect for the old or pity for the young. They will devour the young of your livestock and the crops of your land until you are destroyed. They will leave you no grain, new wine or oil, nor any calves of your herds or lambs of your flocks until you are ruined. They will lay siege to all the cities throughout your land until the high fortified walls in which you trust fall down. They will besiege all the cities throughout the land the Lord your God is giving you. Because of the suffering that your enemy will inflict on you during the siege, you will eat the fruit of the womb, the flesh of the sons and daughters the Lord your God has given you. Even the most gentle and sensitive man among you will have no compassion on his own brother or the wife he loves or his surviving children, and he will not give to one of them any of the flesh of his children that he is eating. It will be all he has left because of the suffering your enemy will inflict on you during the siege of all your cities. The most gentle and sensitive woman among you—so sensitive and gentle that she would not venture to touch the ground with the sole of her foot— will begrudge the husband she loves and her own son or daughter the afterbirth from her womb and the children she bears. For she intends to eat them secretly during the siege and in the distress that your enemy will inflict on you during the siege of your cities. If you do not carefully follow all the words of this law, which are written in this book, and do not revere this glorious and awesome name—the Lord your God— the Lord will send fearful plagues on you and your descendants, harsh and prolonged disasters, and severe and lingering illnesses. He will bring upon you all the diseases of Egypt that you dreaded, and they will cling to you. The Lord will also bring on you every kind of sickness and disaster not recorded in this Book of the Law, until you are destroyed. You who were as numerous as the stars in the sky will be left but few in number, because you did not obey the Lord your God. Just as it pleased the Lord to make you prosper and increase in number, so it will please him to ruin and destroy you. You will be uprooted from the land you are entering to possess. Then the Lord will scatter you among all nations, from one end of the earth to the other. There you will worship other gods—gods of wood and stone, which neither you nor your fathers have known. Among those nations you will find no repose, no resting place for the sole of your foot. There the Lord will give you an anxious mind, eyes weary with longing, and a despairing heart. You will live in constant suspense, filled with dread both night and day, never sure of your life. In the morning you will say, "If only it were evening!" and in the evening, "If only it were morning!"—because of the terror that will fill your hearts and the sights that your eyes will see. The Lord will send you back in ships to Egypt on a journey I said you should never make again. There you will offer yourselves for sale to your enemies as male and female slaves, but no one will buy you. (Deuteronomy 28:15–68 NIV)

God, Creator of all, established obedience as a moral principle from the beginning. Lucifer (aka Satan), formerly one of God's most prized angels, fell to a cursed life when he became proud, and through pride, he entered into self-worship, which led to his disobedience of God. Lucifer and a third of the angels who followed him were cast out of heaven and forever banished from God's kingdom. Pride is one of the major causes of disobedience.

Adam and Eve, the father and mother of all humanity, fell from grace because of their disobedience. God held his creation, mankind, in high esteem, allowing them to share in his power and authority. He blessed Adam and Eve and told them to be fruitful and multiply, to replenish the earth and subdue it, to have dominion over the fish of the sea and over the fowl of the air and over every living thing that moves upon the earth. God also gave them every seed-bearing plant on the face of the earth and every tree that has fruit with seed in it for their food (see Genesis 1:27–29). God planted the garden of Eden and granted Adam responsibility over the garden. Adam was to dress it and to keep it. He expressed to Adam that he may freely eat the fruit from every tree except for the Tree of Knowledge of Good and Evil. Adam was forbidden to eat of that fruit, for if he did, he would surely die (see Genesis 2:15–17). But as life would have it, Satan, the tempter, came along. He tempted Eve (Adam's wife) by getting her to doubt God's instructions, and finally Eve yielded to the temptations and sinned. She disobeyed God by eating the fruit from the Tree of Knowledge of Good and Evil, the very fruit that God forbid them to eat. Adam followed by eating of the fruit as well.

Although many of you reading this book are most likely familiar with Adam and Eve's story, I find it completely appropriate and necessary to highlight their story in this chapter on obedience. By placing the Tree of Knowledge of Good and Evil in the garden, God gave Adam and Eve the freedom to choose to obey or disobey. This wasn't just any tree that they were forbidden to eat the fruit from. This tree was the Tree of Knowledge of Good and Evil. Prior to eating the fruit from this tree, Adam and Eve were innocent, unaware and unashamed of their nakedness. Completely exposed to God, there was nothing they hid from him. However, when temptation came along, they did not seek to turn away from it, but instead they entertained the thought of eating the fruit. In many cases, temptation is subtle, and often it may be difficult to recognize right away. Before long, Eve was overcome by temptation and sinned by disobeying God and eating the fruit from the Tree of Knowledge of Good and Evil. After they ate the fruit from this tree, the husband and wife lost their innocence and gained knowledge of their nakedness and felt guilty about their wrongdoing. Now ashamed and embarrassed of their nakedness, they used fig leaves to cover themselves and then hid in the garden from God.

Just like Adam and Eve, we, too, are given the choice to obey or disobey God. Without a loving and intimate relationship with God, it is impossible to walk in a life of obedience to him. After Adam and Eve sinned by disobeying God's instruction, they gained knowledge that our all-knowing God did not want available to them. (Even after all that God had granted and given to them in the garden of Eden, they still had a want for more. Instead of being thankful for what they had, they sought after what they did not have.) Once they gained the knowledge of good and evil, they began to feel guilty, embarrassed, and ashamed. They hid themselves from God and cut off their communication with him. If we do not communicate with God, then how will we hear or receive his instructions. Without receiving God's instruction and leadership for our lives, it is impossible to obey him. Prior to sinning, their innocence allowed them to walk before God, completely exposed and without any secrets, but their sin took them to a place of secrecy and a lack of trust in their relationship with God. If you cannot trust God, then who do you trust? Who are you sharing your deepest thoughts and secrets with? Is that someone able to deliver you from dark places in your life? Is that someone able to heal you from all sicknesses and diseases? Is that someone all-powerful, all-knowing, omnipresent, righteous, loving, faithful, and just? Is that someone available to you twenty-four hours per day and seven days per week? When we trust God in our relationship with him, we can then patiently await his commands and instructions, which require us to humbly submit and obey all he asks of us.

Adam's Disobedience—Christ's Obedience

When Adam sinned, sin entered the world. Adam's sin brought death, so death spread to everyone, for everyone sinned. Yes, people sinned even before the law was given. But it was not counted as sin because there was not yet any law to break. Still, everyone died—from the time of Adam to the time of Moses—even those who did not disobey an explicit commandment of God, as Adam did. Now Adam is a symbol, a representation of Christ, who was yet to come. But there is a great difference between Adam's sin and God's gracious gift. For the sin of this one man, Adam, brought death to many. But even greater is God's wonderful grace and his gift of forgiveness to many through this other man, Jesus Christ. And the result of God's gracious gift is very different from the result of that one man's sin. For Adam's sin led to condemnation, but God's free gift leads to our being made right with God, even though we are guilty of many sins. For the sin of this one man, Adam, caused death to rule over many. But even greater is God's wonderful grace and his gift of righteousness, for all who receive it will live in triumph over sin and death through this one man, Jesus Christ. Yes, Adam's one sin brings condemnation for everyone, but Christ's one act of righteousness brings a right relationship with God and new life for everyone. Because one person disobeyed God, many became sinners. But because one other person obeyed God, many will be made righteous. (Romans 5:12–19 NLT)

Even when Adam sinned by disobeying God, thereby separating humanity from a right relationship with the Almighty, God, who is full of grace and mercy, already had a plan to restore us back into a right relationship with him, and that plan was through his Son, Jesus Christ.

True Worshippers Obey God

This is what the Lord of Heaven's Armies, the God of Israel, says: "Take your burnt offerings and your other sacrifices and eat them yourselves! When I led your ancestors out of Egypt, it was not burnt offerings and sacrifices I wanted from them. This is what I told them: 'Obey me, and I will be your God, and you will be my people. Do everything as I say, and all will be well!' But my people would not listen to me. They kept doing whatever they wanted, following the stubborn desires of their evil hearts. They went backward instead of forward. From the day your ancestors left Egypt until now, I have continued to send my servants, the prophets—day in and day out. But my people have not listened to me or even tried to hear. They have been stubborn and sinful— even worse than their ancestors. "Tell them all this, but do not expect them to listen. Shout out your warnings, but do not expect them to respond. Say to them, 'This is the nation whose people will not obey the Lord their God and who refuse to be taught. Truth has vanished from among them; it is no longer heard on their lips. Shave your head in mourning, and weep alone on the mountains. For the Lord has rejected and forsaken this generation that has provoked his fury.'" (Jeremiah 7:21–29 NLT)

God called Jeremiah to go stand in the temple gates and warn Judah (God's people) about their false religion and empty religious acts. Their burnt offerings and other sacrifices were being performed for all the wrong reasons. God established sacrifices as a means to show praise, worship, and thankfulness to him. It was also a means for his people to seek him for the forgiveness of their sins and a renewed relationship with Him. The burnt offerings and other sacrifices were all about keeping the heart in right standing with God. God gave specific instructions for the sacrifices, and he required his people's complete submission and obedience to those instructions. Instead of offering sacrifices out of obedience and reverence to their holy God, their sacrifices were being offered out of empty religion and routine religious acts with the hope that God would be pleased with their acts. The exemplary leadership and teachers of the law from Joshua's era were long gone and had since passed away. Less people were being taught true worship and the real importance and purpose of offering sacrifices. Consequently many generations of people forgot God's original plan and purpose for burnt offerings and other sacrifices. They offered sacrifices when and how they supposed might please God instead of obeying God's original instructions and purpose for them. God honors his obedient servants, those who seek and do things his way and not their own way.

Many people today feel as though they have "checked the box" for God because they attended church, gave an offering, tithed, helped the less fortunate, and/or said their prayers. Whether it is Saturday night or Sunday morning worship services, Tuesday or Wednesday night Bible study, or any other times of corporate gathering for worship, many are satisfied with their level of sacrifice for what they feel God requires from them. Although each of these sacrificial acts are wonderful and sacred parts of our worship, we should ask if they are holy and acceptable unto God (see Romans 12:1). In the previous Scripture, we can clearly comprehend that God is looking for our wholehearted worship through obedience. Worshipping God is not something we do once, twice, and maybe three times per week. Worship is not just a religious act, a ceremony, a program, or a service. True worship unto God is a lifestyle of obedience to God. When God speaks, we listen and obey. When God calls, we answer and go.

You may be asking yourself, so how do I begin to live a lifestyle of obedience to God? It all starts with a conversation with God, namely heart-to-heart conversations that grow into communion with God, sparking an intimate and trusting relationship with him. As you continue putting all your trust in God, you find yourself loving him and submitting to his lordship and bearing all your deepest thoughts and secrets to Him, your Lord and Master. So when your Master speaks, you are more than willing to hear and obey his commands. His will becomes far more important than your own desires and will. Through obedience, your sacrifices are holy and acceptable to him.

> And so, dear brothers and sisters, I plead with you to give your bodies to God because of all he has done for you. Let them be a living and holy sacrifice—the kind he will find acceptable. This is truly the way to worship him. Don't copy the behavior and customs of this world, but let God transform you into a new person by changing the way you think. Then you will learn to know God's will for you, which is good and pleasing and perfect. (Romans 12:1–2 NLT)

Behold, To Obey Is Better than Sacrifice

> Samuel said to Saul, "I am the one the Lord sent to anoint you king over his people Israel; so listen now to the message from the Lord. This is what the Lord Almighty says: 'I will punish the Amalekites for what they did to Israel when they waylaid them as they came up from Egypt. Now go, attack the Amalekites and totally destroy

everything that belongs to them. Do not spare them; put to death men and women, children and infants, cattle and sheep, camels and donkeys.'" So Saul summoned the men and mustered them at Telaim—two hundred thousand foot soldiers and ten thousand from Judah. Saul went to the city of Amalek and set an ambush in the ravine. Then he said to the Kenites, "Go away, leave the Amalekites so that I do not destroy you along with them; for you showed kindness to all the Israelites when they came up out of Egypt." So the Kenites moved away from the Amalekites. Then Saul attacked the Amalekites all the way from Havilah to Shur, to the east of Egypt. He took Agag king of the Amalekites alive, and all his people he totally destroyed with the sword. But Saul and the army spared Agag and the best of the sheep and cattle, the fat calves and lambs—everything that was good. These they were unwilling to destroy completely, but everything that was despised and weak they totally destroyed. Then the word of the Lord came to Samuel: "I am grieved that I have made Saul king, because he has turned away from me and has not carried out my instructions." Samuel was troubled, and he cried out to the Lord all that night. Early in the morning Samuel got up and went to meet Saul, but he was told, "Saul has gone to Carmel. There he has set up a monument in his own honor and has turned and gone on down to Gilgal." When Samuel reached him, Saul said, "The Lord bless you! I have carried out the Lord's instructions." But Samuel said, "What then is this bleating of sheep in my ears? What is this lowing of cattle that I hear?" Saul answered, "The soldiers brought them from the Amalekites; they spared the best of the sheep and cattle to sacrifice to the Lord your God, but we totally destroyed the rest." "Stop!" Samuel said to Saul. "Let me tell you what the Lord said to me last night." "Tell me," Saul replied. Samuel said, "Although you were once small in your own eyes, did you not become the head of the tribes of Israel? The Lord anointed you king over Israel. And he sent you on a mission, saying, 'Go and completely destroy those wicked people, the Amalekites; make war on them until you have wiped them out.' Why did you not obey the Lord? Why did you pounce on the plunder and do evil in the eyes of the Lord?" "But I did obey the Lord," Saul said. "I went on the mission the Lord assigned me. I completely destroyed the Amalekites and brought back Agag their king. The soldiers took sheep and cattle from the plunder, the best of what was devoted to God, in order to sacrifice them to the Lord your God at Gilgal." But Samuel replied: "Does the Lord delight in burnt offerings and sacrifices as much as in obeying the voice of the Lord? To obey is better than sacrifice, and to heed is better than the fat of rams. For rebellion is like the sin of divination, and arrogance like the evil of idolatry. Because you have rejected the word of the Lord, he has rejected you as king." (1 Samuel 15:1–23 NIV)

We hear the Scripture, "To obey is better than sacrifice," quoted all the time, but how many of us really understand its significance and take heed? In essence, the Scripture is telling us that obedience to God far outweighs all other ceremonial forms of worship. God does not need our worship. Instead we need to worship God through obedience. He established worship as a way for us to humble ourselves and come before him with loving and upright hearts, thankfulness, and faithfulness. God honors true worship from the heart.

For Saul, he disobeyed God's instructions and used sacrificing to the Lord as an excuse for his own selfish and greedy motives. He glossed right over his sin of disobedience for the sake of his own personal gain and interests. God knows us better than we know ourselves. He knows our hearts and the motives of our hearts, so no matter how much we may think we are kidding God, we are only kidding ourselves. God is the only one able to read the heart of man.

Disobedience is a form of rebellion. The last verse compares rebellion to the sin of divination (witchcraft), a sin worthy of death, as it ended up costing Saul his throne as Israel's king. Furthermore, as we see in the previous passages, God said to Samuel, "I regret that I have made Saul king, because he has turned away from me and has not carried out my instructions" (see 1 Samuel 15:11). Turning away from God to do things our own way and in our own timing gives birth to spiritual disasters and calamities. God knew Saul's heart could no longer be trusted for leading his people (Israel). Therefore, the Lord rejected Saul as king.

CHAPTER 8

Patience

Patience is having the ability to endure when difficult circumstances arise. This gives us the capacity to suppress our restlessness, temper, or irritableness when we are faced with delay, pain, mishaps, or provocation.

Patience is a character value within us that must be learned and developed from the time we are born. As newborn babies, we are not willing to wait very long for our feedings. Our little tummies signal to our brains that we are hungry and need food. Our brains then rapidly send the message all over our little bodies. Our mouths immediately begin searching for the food source. When we don't find one, our little feet begin kicking. Our hands and fingers move about, and within minutes if we haven't received food, we begin crying until the food is brought. Even as babies, some of us are born with a little more patience to wait without complaint or irritation than others. Children/babies who learn patience very early lend ease to the parenting process, making Mom and Dad's lives much more enjoyable.

In this chapter, we will learn that patience is a necessary character trait we need working in us as we walk out our relationship with God. Growing in a relationship with God requires us to increase in patience through his Holy Spirit. In Christ, patience is a form of spiritual maturity. If we strive to live for God, we must learn to wait for God … he leads, we follow.

In the early establishment of our relationship with God, we learn quickly that *he is* who he says he is, he does what he says he will do, and his faithfulness is beyond our imagination. This enables us to put great trust in him. If we trust him, we can then look to him for guidance and instructions. When we pray and talk to God about our deepest concerns, we must recognize God is faithful, and he will respond. His responses and guidance are not based on our own will and timetable though. They are based on God's will and timing for each of our lives. He is all-knowing, and his timing is perfect. If you want God to lead your life, learn to patiently wait on him concerning all things. Hebrews 10:36 (KJV) says, "For ye have need of patience, that, after ye have done the will of God, ye might receive the promise."

Patience Is a Virtue

Patience is a virtue. It's a proverbial phrase or cliché we are all familiar with. Although many believe that the phrase itself originated from the "Piers Plowman" poem written in the fourteenth century, patience (aka long-suffering) is a character trait of God's own Spirit (see Galatians 5:22–23, which talks about the fruit of the Holy Spirit). For that reason alone, we must acknowledge that patience is a virtuous character quality highly esteemed by God. Being made in the likeness of his own image, patience is a virtue (from the Holy Spirit) that we all must embrace and walk in. But many of us struggle with upholding the character quality of patience in our lives.

What is it about patience that we struggle with? Why do we have difficulty maintaining it in our lives? Patience is described as an ability or willingness to suppress anxiety or irritations because of delay, pain, mishap, or provocation. In other words, patience causes us to wait during a time or situation that is contrary to our own will, way, or comfort level. Our own will desires to maintain control. It wants what it wants when it wants it, and it does what it wants to do when, where, and how it pleases. The real struggle begins when patience comes along and gives our self-will a moral pushback, saying "No, now is not the time," or, "No, that's not the path to be taken or how it should be done." Our ego, which drives our will, then begins to feel a certain way (restless, annoyed, irritated, etc.). Those with no patience will allow their ego to take charge and handle the situation according to its own will and way. However, those who have developed the virtue of patience will decrease in their flesh and allow the Holy Spirit within to rise and bring peace into the situation by getting the ego to trust and submit to another way—in this case, God's way. As Christians, patience motivates us to yield to God's will, ways, and timing, thereby producing a victorious and successful life.

God's Thoughts and Ways

"My thoughts are nothing like your thoughts,"
says the Lord.
"And my ways are far beyond anything you could
imagine."
For just as the heavens are higher than the earth,
so my ways are higher than your ways
and my thoughts higher than your thoughts."
"The rain and snow come down from the heavens
and stay on the ground to water the earth.
They cause the grain to grow,
producing seed for the farmer
and bread for the hungry.
It is the same with my word.
I send it out, and it always produces fruit.
It will accomplish all I want it to,
and it will prosper everywhere I send it.
You will live in joy and peace.
The mountains and hills will burst into song,
and the trees of the field will clap their hands!
Where once there were thorns, cypress trees will
grow.
Where nettles grew, myrtles will sprout up.
These events will bring great honor to the Lord's
name;
they will be an everlasting sign of his power and
love."
(Isaiah 55:8–13 NLT)

God's thoughts and ways are much greater than ours. He is an infinite God. He has no limits, no boundaries. Therefore, his thoughts and ways are without limits and boundaries. We (mankind) were made by God in the likeness of his image, but we are finite (limited) in our capacity to think and use our abilities. The almighty God reigns supreme in every way. He is our go-to authority concerning all matters. The wicked choose their own thoughts and ways, but the righteous look to the supreme ways and thoughts of God for guidance. Seeking God's thoughts and ways yield a long life of peace and prosperity. Matthew 6:33 (NKJV) tells us, "But seek first the kingdom of God and His righteousness, and all these things shall be added to you."

Are we willing to suppress our restlessness, annoyances, and irritations by trusting God's thoughts and ways over our own with the understanding that what he says (his Word) will not return to him void but will accomplish that which he commanded? God's thoughts, ways, plans, and timing are perfect in every way, and if we wait on him, he will faithfully deliver. Patience produces a peaceful and worry-free atmosphere. God may not come when you want him, but he's always on time. Our walk with God requires patience, and patience is developed through the testing of our faith. "My brethren, count it all joy when you fall into various trials, knowing that the testing of your faith produces patience. But let patience have its perfect work, that you may be perfect and complete, lacking nothing" (James 1:2–4 NKJV). "God blesses those who patiently endure testing and temptation. Afterward they will receive the crown of life that God has promised to those who love him" (James 1:12 NLT).

Testing Our Faith

May I remind you that "as children of God, through our faith we victoriously overcome this evil world" (see 1 John 5:4). Because of this simple but very important truth, it is a necessity that our faith be tested. By way of his Spirit, God will see to it that we are equipped to endure to the end. Life tests and trials strengthen us in our faith and develop our patience so that we can endure. If we want to live for God, patience must be an essential fruit of our very own spirit.

Mary and Martha's faith was truly tested during the sickness and death of their brother, Lazarus.

> Now a man named Lazarus was sick. He was from Bethany, the village of Mary and her sister Martha. This Mary, whose brother Lazarus now lay sick, was the same one who poured perfume on the Lord and wiped his feet with her hair. So the sisters sent word to Jesus, "Lord, the one you love is sick." When he heard this, Jesus said, "This sickness will not end in death. No, it is for God's glory so that God's Son may be glorified through it." Jesus loved Martha and her sister and Lazarus. Yet when he heard that Lazarus was sick, he stayed where he was two more days. Then he said to his disciples, "Let us go back to Judea." "But Rabbi," they said, "a short while ago the Jews tried to stone you, and yet you are going back there?" Jesus answered, "Are there not twelve hours of daylight? A man who walks by day will not stumble, for he sees by this

world's light. It is when he walks by night that the stumbles, for he has no light." After he had said this, he went on to tell them, "Our friend Lazarus has fallen asleep; but I am going there to wake him up." His disciples replied, "Lord, if he sleeps, he will get better." Jesus had been speaking of his death, but his disciples thought he meant natural sleep. So then he told them plainly, "Lazarus is dead, and for your sake I am glad I was not there, so that you may believe. But let us go to him." Then Thomas (called Didymus) said to the rest of the disciples, "Let us also go, that we may die with him." On his arrival, Jesus found that Lazarus had already been in the tomb for four days. Bethany was less than two miles from Jerusalem, and many Jews had come to Martha and Mary to comfort them in the loss of their brother. When Martha heard that Jesus was coming, she went out to meet him, but Mary stayed at home. "Lord," Martha said to Jesus, "if you had been here, my brother would not have died. But I know that even now God will give you whatever you ask." Jesus said to her, "Your brother will rise again."

Martha answered, "I know he will rise again in the resurrection at the last day." Jesus said to her, "I am the resurrection and the life. He who believes in me will live, even though he dies; and whoever lives and believes in me will never die. Do you believe this?" "Yes, Lord," she told him, "I believe that you are the Christ, the Son of God, who was to come into the world." After she had said this, she went back and called her sister Mary aside. "The Teacher is here," she said, "and is asking for you." When Mary heard this, she got up quickly and went to him. Now Jesus had not yet entered the village, but was still at the place where Martha had met him. When the Jews who had been with Mary in the house, comforting her, noticed how quickly she got up and went out, they followed her, supposing she was going to the tomb to mourn there. When Mary reached the place where Jesus was and saw him, she fell at his feet and said, "Lord, if you had been here, my brother would not have died." When Jesus saw her weeping, and the Jews who had come along with her also weeping, he was deeply moved in spirit and troubled. "Where have you laid him?" he asked. "Come and see, Lord," they replied. Jesus wept. Then the Jews said, "See how he loved him!" But some of them said, "Could not he who opened the eyes of the blind man have kept this man from dying?" Jesus, once more deeply moved, came to the tomb. It was a cave with a stone laid across the entrance. "Take away the stone," he said. "But, Lord," said Martha, the sister of the dead man, "by this time there is a bad odor, for he has been there four days." Then Jesus said, "Did I not tell you that if you believe, you would see the glory of God?" So they took away the stone. Then Jesus looked up and said, "Father, I thank you that you have heard me. I knew that you always hear me, but I said this for the benefit of the people standing here, that they may believe that you sent me." When he had said this, Jesus called in a loud voice, "Lazarus, come out!" The dead man came out, his hands and feet wrapped with strips of linen, and a cloth around his face. Jesus said to them, "Take off the grave clothes and let him go." (John 11:1–44 NIV)

As followers of Jesus Christ, the two sisters were well aware of Jesus's power to heal the sick and raise the dead. So they sent a message to Jesus that their brother, Lazarus, a friend and follower of Christ himself, was sick. Note that Mary and Martha's message did not tell Jesus what to do, but instead it informed Jesus of their situation and concerns. Jesus received the message but decided to remain where he was for two additional days before he headed back to their village. For Mary and Martha, this must have been a great challenge and test of their faith, watching their brother through his sickness and then finally his death. How many times have we prayed and interceded on behalf of family, friends, and others? How many times did it seem like God was nowhere in the mix or was not answering our prayers immediately? A very vital part of our faith walk with God is possessing the faith to wait on him. Again in Isaiah 55:8–9, God tells us that our thoughts are nothing like his thoughts. Nor are our ways his ways, for his ways and thoughts are higher than our ways and thoughts. With that said, we must know that God works in his own timing for all situations. He's never late but always right on time. Just as Jesus received Mary and Martha's message, he hears the prayers of God's children. Only God knows what is best, and we must maintain our faith in him and his timing. Even when situations are at their worst and not going as you expected (i.e., the loss of a loved one, a permanent injury, an eviction from your house, bankruptcy, etc.), our faith must carry us through. Our faith tells us that God's way is the better way, giving all thanks and glory to him.

Although Lazarus had been dead for four days, Jesus's arrival was right on time. Both Mary and Martha stated to Jesus, "Lord, if only you had been here, our brother would not have died." They were essentially saying, "Lord, you're late!" This kind of thinking comes from our limited human thoughts and not the thoughts of our higher-thinking God. Death is our final enemy, but with God, all things are possible (see Matthew 19:26). Jesus's response to Martha was the assurance that her brother, Lazarus, would rise again. Martha did not really grasp the impact of what he said, so Jesus said to her, "I am the resurrection and the life" (John 11:25 NKJV). The resurrection power of Jesus Christ is the key to our faith. Through Jesus's resurrection power, death now has no sting. Jesus goes on to say, "He who believes in Me, though he may die, he shall live. And whoever lives and believes in Me shall never die" (John 11:25–26 NKJV). In other words, when we put all of our faith in Jesus Christ, who assures us he is the resurrection and the life, we shall have the victory (live) over all enemies, including death.

As you can see from the text, Martha still had faith in Jesus's power. It was the timing that had her distressed. Waiting on God is one of the greatest challenges that believers face in their walk. Put yourself in the place of Mary and Martha. How might you have handled the situation? Would you have patiently waited for the Lord to respond so that the situation is handled his way and not your own way? It is cases like this with Lazarus's death and many others throughout the Bible (such as Daniel thrown into a pit with lions) that assist us with our personal spiritual growth and teach us God's faithfulness to respond to our prayers. Through faith we must learn to wait on the Lord. He may not respond when we want, but he is always on time.

By Faith, Patience Is Produced

Abram (later God changed to Abraham), a man of great faith, lived a life of believing and obeying God's every command. He was well in his years when God called him to leave his family and relatives in Haran and move to Canaan.

> The Lord had said to Abram, "Leave your native country, your relatives, and your father's family, and go to the land that I will show you. I will make you into a great nation. I will bless you and make you famous, and you will be a blessing to others. I will bless those who bless you and curse those who treat you with contempt. All the families on earth will be blessed through you." So Abram departed as the Lord had instructed, and Lot went with him. Abram was seventy-five years old when he left Haran. He took his wife, Sarai, his nephew Lot, and all his wealth—his livestock and all the people he had taken into his household at Haran—and headed for the land of Canaan. When they arrived in Canaan, Abram traveled through the land as far as Shechem. There he set up camp beside the oak of Moreh. At that time, the area was inhabited by Canaanites. Then the

Lord appeared to Abram and said, "I will give this land to your descendants." And Abram built an altar there and dedicated it to the Lord, who had appeared to him. After that, Abram traveled south and set up camp in the hill country, with Bethel to the west and Ai to the east. There he built another altar and dedicated it to the Lord, and he worshiped the Lord. Then Abram continued traveling south by stages toward the Negev. (Genesis 12:1–9 NLT)

At the age of seventy-five, Abram stepped out on faith and obeyed as God instructed. God promised Abram that he would make him into a great and blessed nation, a blessed nation that would represent God's love and power and bring influence to other nations with whom it came in contact. Abram (Abraham), known as "the father of our faith," set the standard for our faith walk. As Abraham's descendants, we, too, must submit to following God's divine instructions, even if it requires our moving away from the familiar and going toward the unfamiliar.

Sometime later God made a covenant with Abram, promising that he would have a son of his own and be the father of many nations. Many years preceding the Lord's covenant promise, Abram walked in obedience to God. Although Abram's obedience was a direct result of his faith, it was his trusting and believing heart (faith) that made him righteous in the eyes of God. "And Abram believed the Lord, and the Lord counted him as righteous because of his faith" (Genesis 15:6 NLT).

Without faith, it is impossible to please God (see Hebrews 11:6). For so many of us, we get caught up in thinking we must live a flawless and "holier than thou" life in order to be accepted by God, but this reasoning is far from the truth. It is our faith that makes us righteous. God justifies us by our faith in him. "Therefore, since we have been made right in God's sight by faith, we have peace with God because of what Jesus Christ our Lord has done for us. Because of our faith, Christ has brought us into this place of undeserved privilege where we now stand, and we confidently and joyfully look forward to sharing God's glory" (Romans 5:1–2 NLT).

Abram believed God for the unseen and not the seen. He already possessed great wealth and fame. However, it was descendants that Abram lacked, and God saw to it that this need was met. God promises that the needs of his people shall be met. At this point in Abram's life, he is well into his seventies, and his wife is well past childbearing years. Nonetheless, Abram believed what God said, and he believed that God would do just what he said he would do. When God makes a promise or gives us insight on what he is going to do, we must know that God will deliver. He says "His word will not return to him void, it will accomplish that which he sends it to do" (see Isaiah 55:11).

At the age of ninety-nine, God appeared to Abram and repeated his promise to him, this time adding further details in preparation of executing his promise. A short while before the promised son was conceived, God changed Abram's name to Abraham (meaning the "father of many nations"). He also changed Abraham's wife Sarai's name to Sarah (meaning the "mother of nations"), clearly showing that Sarah shall bear

Abraham a son named Isaac, in whom he will establish his everlasting covenant. In hearing God's confirmation that he and his wife, Sarah, would birth a child at their ripe old ages of a hundred years and ninety years respectively, he fell out laughing and wondered within himself how this could be since they both were very old. Although Abraham experienced doubt concerning God's promise, he continued to believe God from his heart and acted accordingly, accepting the terms and conditions of the covenant and obeying God's instructions concerning the covenant. Just like Abraham, we, too, may doubt the miraculous power of God working on our behalf. However, we serve an extraordinary God who blesses his children and executes his promises in unconventional ways. It was Abraham's faith that produced the patience to wait out the promise of God. By faith, Abraham waited twenty-five years for God's promise to manifest. In our personal relationship with God, he speaks and reveals his promises for our lives; however, it is our duty to remain in communion with him and patiently wait to receive all terms and conditions. "Wait on the Lord; be of good courage, and He shall strengthen your heart; wait, I say, on the Lord" (see Psalm 27:14 NKJV).

Patiently Waiting on the Lord

Several years prior to starting Eye on the Prize Ministries International, the Holy Spirit spoke to me and said I would have a ministry, and the name would be "Eye on the Prize Ministries." I heard the Lord, though I did not know how it would come to pass, I believed him and wrote the name in my journal. I did not share this information with anyone. It was a covenant promise between God and me. By faith, I journeyed with God, allowing him to prepare me through considerable amounts of testing, impartation, and studying his Word. After nine years of patiently waiting, God spoke, "I'm calling you now, daughter. Start the ministry," and it was so. It is amazing to me how nine years went by from the time he first spoke the promise to the time he called me to execute or birth the promise. It is through my journey (faith walk) with God that I have learned to patiently wait on him. "But they that wait upon the Lord shall renew their strength; they shall mount up with wings as eagles; they shall run, and not be weary; and they shall walk, and not faint" (Isaiah 40:31 KJV).

Although we may grow tired and weary during the journey, it is essential that we learn to wait on the Lord, not moving ahead of his plan for our own convenience. He is the source of our strength, so pray and ask him to renew your strength. "He is our shield and exceedingly great reward" (see Genesis 15:1). In other words, he protects us during the times of struggle, and he is faithful to deliver on his great blessings promised. Patiently waiting on the Lord develops virtuous characters in us, which in turn bring peace, love, hope, and joy in our lives as well as the lives of others.

Testing Our Patience—Patience in the Midst of the Storm or Crisis

When walking by faith, our patience stands to be tested. It's one thing to have our faith tested, especially when we know that the trying of our faith produces patience, but what about when our patience is then put to the test? The testing of our patience determines just how solid we are in our wait. How long can we withstand forces and pressures put upon us before we give up (crack) and give in (crumble) under those pressures? Here we will learn about a man known to many Christians for his faith and patience, one who persevered through a season of great tests and trials.

There was a man in the land of Uz, whose name was Job; and that man was blameless and upright, and one who feared God and shunned evil. And seven sons and three daughters were born to him. Also, his possessions were seven thousand sheep, three thousand camels, five hundred yoke of oxen, five hundred female donkeys, and a very large household, so that this man was the greatest of all the people of the East. And his sons would go and feast in their houses, each on his appointed day, and would send and invite their three sisters to eat and drink with them. So it was, when the days of feasting had run their course, that Job would send and sanctify them, and he would rise early in the morning and offer burnt offerings according to the number of them all. For Job said, "It may be that my sons have sinned and cursed God in their hearts." Thus Job did regularly.

Now there was a day when the sons of God came to present themselves before the Lord, and Satan also came among them. And the Lord said to Satan, "From where do you come?"

So Satan answered the Lord and said, "From going to and fro on the earth, and from walking back and forth on it." Then the Lord said to Satan, "Have you considered My servant Job, that there is none like him on the earth, a blameless and upright man, one who fears God and shuns evil?" So Satan answered the Lord and said, "Does Job fear God for nothing? Have You not made a hedge around him, around his household, and around all that he has on every side? You have blessed the work of his hands, and his possessions have increased in the land. But now, stretch out Your hand and touch all that he has, and he will surely curse You to Your face!" And the Lord said to Satan, "Behold, all that he has is in your power; only do not lay a hand on his person." So Satan went out from the presence of the Lord.

Now there was a day when his sons and daughters were eating and drinking wine in their oldest brother's house; and a messenger came to Job and said, "The oxen were plowing and the donkeys feeding beside them, when the Sabeans raided them and took them away—indeed they have killed the servants with the edge of the sword; and I alone have escaped to tell you!" While he was still speaking, another also came and said, "The fire of God fell from heaven and burned up the sheep and the servants, and consumed them; and I alone have escaped to tell you!" While he was still speaking, another also came and said,

"The Chaldeans formed three bands, raided the camels and took them away, yes, and killed the servants with the edge of the sword; and I alone have escaped to tell you!" While he was still speaking, another also came and said, "Your sons and daughters were eating and drinking wine in their oldest brother's house, and suddenly a great wind came from across the wilderness and struck the four corners of the house, and it fell on the young people, and they are dead; and I alone have escaped to tell you!" Then Job arose, tore his robe, and shaved his head; and he fell to the ground and worshiped. And he said:

"Naked I came from my mother's womb, And naked shall I return there. The Lord gave, and the Lord has taken away; Blessed be the name of the Lord." In all this Job did not sin nor charge God with wrong. (Job 1:1–22 NKJV)

Job was a wealthy and upright man, a man who trusted, obeyed, and worshipped God faithfully. Although wealthy and blessed in every area of his life, Job kept God first and foremost in his life. With his heart pure and spirit humbled, Job did not allow his possessions to interfere with his relationship with God. Job was truly a model citizen of faith who lived for God. And because of his faith, Satan (the Enemy) sought to accuse and attack him. However, the Enemy cannot touch or much less destroy God's people without permission from God. (Satan is real. In fact, he was originally one of God's prize angels who later became corrupt and rebellious through pride. His pride led him to rebel against God, and as a result, he was kicked out of heaven.)

Satan came before God, accusing Job of having faith and loving God only because God had blessed him with many possessions and because things were going well in his life. Satan claimed if Job lost all that he had, he would become angry and curse God. God then allowed Satan to destroy all of Job's possessions, including his children, but Satan was not permitted to touch or destroy Job. When you are facing an attack or spiritual warfare in your life, always remember that the Enemy can only go as far as God allows. Remain prayerful, and ask others (whom you trust) to pray for you and with you.

When Job received the news of all these egregious attacks upon his life, he stood up, tore his robe, shaved his head, fell to the ground, and worshipped God. Although Job outwardly expressed his heartache and emotions toward the loss of his loved ones, he also recognized that even in the midst of his testing and trials, God was still sovereign and all-powerful. His mercy would endure forever. Job did not turn against God out of anger but instead turned to God for comfort.

In 2011, I was diagnosed with breast cancer, but instead of looking to myself and others for a solution, I lifted my eyes up to God's holy hill and took the case before him. I knew that God was my healer and that the cancer cells could only go as far as God permitted. Miraculously the one centimeter lump sat right on top of my lymph nodes, but the cells stayed within a half-inch margin, not moving any farther than God would allow. I did not ask, "Why me, Lord?" Instead I thanked God for the test and asked him to give me the strength and patience to walk through the journey victoriously. Through his Word, God spoke many reassuring Scriptures that told me I was going to be okay and that I would not die but live (see Psalm 118:17).

In Job 2, Satan again came before God, accusing Job of only loving God because of his blessed life. He argued that although Job grieved over the loss of his loved ones and possessions, he continued to proclaim his life as blessed because God allowed him to escape and not experience personal pain. So Satan asked God if he could touch and physically afflict Job. God could see right through Satan's plan and attempt to manipulate. But God went ahead and gave him permission to physically afflict Job; however, Satan was not allowed to destroy Job. God has full control over the Enemy's attacks. The Enemy can only go where God has permitted. If God has the power and authority to permit the attack, he surely has the power and authority to save and deliver you from being devoured. There may be times when we don't comprehend the reason or the season for our sufferings, but if we put our trust in God, we shall make it through. "Yea, though I walk through the valley of the shadow of death, I will fear no evil; for (You) are with me; Your rod and Your staff, they comfort me" (Psalm 23:4 KJV). God is with us during the good times as well as times of trials and suffering.

After the Enemy physically afflicted Job with agonizing, painful boils on his skin that stretched from head to toe, Job sat down among the ashes in great mourning and humility. While Job suffered in overwhelming pain, his wife mocked his faith by saying, "Are you still trying to maintain your integrity? Curse

God and die" (see Job 2:9 NLT). As believers, we are not exempt from pain and sufferings. In fact, our sufferings may at times be greater than that of unbelievers. Satan (our Enemy) seeks to drive a wedge between us and God by tempting us to sin against God.

It must have been extremely disheartening for Job to learn that the person (his wife) who should have comforted him lost all faith and encouraged him to give up his faith and commit suicide. Even through this agonizing physical affliction and disappointment, Job did not curse God.

Finally Job's friends come to visit him. At the sight of Job's condition, his friends were mortified, but they kept silent. They mourned with him for seven days before the silence was broken by Job. With opinions already formed in their own minds, they begin arguing each of their points with Job as to why he must go through the suffering. Their arguments brought even more grief rather than comfort to Job. After a long and drawn- out debate among Job and his friends, God finally spoke to Job. He confronted Job by setting the record straight concerning his great power and authority over all the heavens and earth. Although God knew the purpose for Job's sufferings, he was not obligated in any way to explain himself. God is not a tormenter that runs around causing unnecessary pain and suffering. He is merciful, righteous, and just to all. He reminded Job to be content even when he did not know the reason for his sufferings. When we don't understand the *why*, trusting God in everything gives us the faith we need to patiently endure the storm.

In the end, Job maintained uprightness in the eyes of God, and he blessed Job and restored his family and possessions back to him. Job's wealth was much greater than his former prosperity too.

Patience is about maintaining a steadfast focus on God even in the midst of our worst turmoil. Patience is a character quality embraced by steadfast servants in the Lord.

CHAPTER 9

Humility

In chapter 6, we learned that a pure heart is a character value necessary for God to trust us with his resources and assignments. The motives of the pure at heart are untainted and selfless in nature. When our hearts are pure, we think pure thoughts and unceasingly yield our spirit to the will and ways of God. Out of a pure heart comes true humility. True humility is achieved when we can let go of the self (self-credit, self-focus, self-thoughts, self-pride, self-ways, etc.) and recognize the greater importance or rank of God and/or others. When our spirit is humbled toward God, we recognize his sovereignty and are at peace with yielding to his lordship over our lives, giving God all the glory and praise for our accomplishments.

Humility is a state of mind. It is not something we can achieve on our own. We need the work of God's Holy Spirit to show us just how weak and insignificant we are without Him. God is our Creator, who graciously gave us every gift of wisdom, knowledge, talent, ability, and wealth that we possess. God is the Source of our resources, but he gives us the free will to choose the usage and administration of those resources. How will you choose?

Will you use your gifts and wealth for your own edification and gain, or are you willing to humble yourself and use your gifts and talents for the glory of God? In living a life for God, there is no room for pride. Humility becomes the primary state of our mind. Self-cares and concerns yield to God's cares and concerns. "For it is God who works in you both to will and to do for His good pleasure" (Philippians 2:13 NKJV).

> Now a man came up to Jesus and asked, "Teacher, what good thing must I do to get eternal life?" "Why do you ask me about what is good?" Jesus replied. "There is only One who is good. If you want to enter life, obey the commandments." "Which ones?" the man inquired. Jesus replied, "'Do not murder, do not commit adultery, do not steal, do not give false testimony, honor your father and mother,' and 'love your neighbor as yourself.'" "All these I have kept," the young man said. "What do I still lack?" Jesus answered, "If you want to be perfect, go, sell your possessions and give to the poor, and you will have treasure in heaven. Then come, follow me." When the young man heard this, he went away sad, because he had great wealth. Then Jesus said to his disciples, "I tell you the truth, it is hard for a rich man to enter the kingdom of heaven. Again I tell you, it is easier for a camel to go through the eye of a needle than for a rich man to enter the kingdom of God." When the disciples heard this, they were greatly astonished and asked, "Who then can be saved?" Jesus looked at them and said,

"With man this is impossible, but with God all things are possible." Peter answered him, "We have left everything to follow you! What then will there be for us? Jesus said to them, "I tell you the truth, at the renewal of all things, when the Son of Man sits on his glorious throne, you who have followed me will also sit on twelve thrones, judging the twelve tribes of Israel. And everyone who has left houses or brothers or sisters or father or mother or children or fields for my sake will receive a hundred times as much and will inherit eternal life. But many who are first will be last, and many who are last will be first. (Matthew 19:16–30 NIV)

Many people think this story is about God rejecting the financially rich, but instead it is about God rejecting the proud. The man who happened to be wealthy asked Jesus what good deed he must do to get eternal life. Immediately Jesus gave God the glory, saying, "There is only One who is good, and if you want eternal life, you must hearken and obey His commandments." The man then boasted that he had kept all the commandments and then asked what else he had to do. Jesus informed the man that if he really wanted to be complete in God, he must go sell all his possessions and give the money to the poor. Then he would have treasure in heaven. This request is where the rubber met the road. The man was not willing to submit to this request. Because of his pride, he was not willing to go down to absolutely nothing—no roof over his head, no livestock, no education, no family, no friends, not a single possession but God. He was proud of his possessions and the accomplishments that he had so successfully achieved for himself. I'm sure friends, family, and associates near and far looked up to him because of all that he had done. He had made a name for himself, and now it was in jeopardy of being taken away. Verse 22 says, "When the young man heard this, he went away sad, because he had great wealth." In other words, he stood to lose everything that he thought was his in exchange for eternal life. This is precisely the price we must pay to receive our treasure in heaven (eternal life). To give up or to lose everything does not necessarily mean losing all your possessions here on earth physically, although it could; however, it does means that you have resolved in your heart that nothing (not anything you own) is as important as God and his lordship in your life. Everything we possess here on earth is only temporary. We cannot take anything with us when we die. It is also important for us to comprehend that all wealth (knowledge, material items, finances, family, health, etc.) we have accumulated was given by God, even if your house is a tent and a rusty wheelbarrow is your transportation. Nothing belongs to us. Everything belongs to God.

After the man of wealth walked away, unable to find the humility in his heart to sell all his possessions for an eternal life in Christ, Jesus turned to his followers and said, "I tell you the truth, it is hard for a rich man to enter the kingdom of heaven. Again I tell you, it is easier for a camel to go through the eye of a needle than for a rich man to enter the kingdom of God" (Matthew 19:23–24 NIV). His disciples were shocked when they heard this and asked him, "Then who can be saved?" Jesus sternly looked at them and said, "Humanly speaking, it is impossible, but with God, all things are possible" (Matthew 19:26 NLT).

All power belongs to God, and until man (humanity) can realize he really has no real power and can humble himself under the mighty power of God (see 1 Peter 5:6), he can never make it into God's kingdom. Without lowering ourselves, we can never become followers of Christ and receive eternal life. "God is opposed to the proud, but gives grace to the humble" (see 1 Peter 5:5 NASB). The proud are self-absorbed, but the humble are lowly and yielding in spirit. As soon as we take the self out and remove the human side, God can have full charge. That's why Jesus said, "With man, it is impossible, but with God, all things are possible." Jesus reassured his followers that there is treasure in heaven for them, and all followers who give up all their worldly possessions for his sake will receive so much more and will inherit eternal life.

In the previous Scripture passage Jesus states that it is hard for a rich man to enter the kingdom of heaven. He is referring to one who is wealthy (i.e., abundance in possessions, finances, health, education/knowledge, and any other life accomplishments and achievements). Although God welcomes and even promises wealth for our lives, he does not welcome the pride that may come with it. It is God who gives us the power to get wealth. Deuteronomy 8:18 (NKJV) says, "And you shall remember the Lord your God, for it is He who gives you power to get wealth, that He may establish His covenant which He swore to your fathers, as it is this day." When we humbly recognize that everything that we possess is because of God's free gift of grace and mercy, including our salvation, we can then become fit for living in God's kingdom.

In the previous chapter, we learned just how humble Job was when he removed the spotlight from his own life and shed his possessions and gave all honor and glory to God. Job, an upright servant of God, endured a severe attack from Satan that resulted in the loss all his possessions. Job knew that everything he had here on earth did not permanently belong to him, but it was all by the grace of God. When Job received the news that Satan struck down all his possessions, he stood up, tore his robe, fell to the ground (which means he humbled himself), and gave all honor and glory to God. He was not concerned about his stuff. He was more concerned about still trusting God in his life. He said, "I came naked from my mother's womb, and I will be naked when I leave. The Lord gave me what I had, and the Lord has taken it away. Praise the name of the Lord" (Job 1:21 NLT).

It is when we are at that lowest (humiliating) point in our lives that God opens the eyes of our true understanding and we realize we are nothing without him. You thought you knew it all. You thought you had all your personal and family matters under control. You thought your business and career were rock solid. You didn't think you needed a hand in anything—that is, until life dealt you a blow that caused you to recognize your true weakness and mortal flesh and blood. God wants you to know he is merciful. Even after you live a life filled with pride, when you find deep within your heart to humble yourself, God will pick you up. "So humble yourselves under the mighty power of God, and at the right time he will lift you up in honor" (1 Peter 5:6 NLT).

Humility Saves Nations

God appeared to Solomon that very night and said, "I accept your prayer; yes, I have chosen this place as a temple for sacrifice, a house of worship. If I ever shut off the supply of rain from the skies or order the locusts to eat the crops or send a plague on my people, and my people, my God-defined people, respond by humbling themselves, praying, seeking my presence, and turning their backs on their wicked lives, I'll be there ready for you: I'll listen from heaven, forgive their sins, and restore their land to health. From now on I'm alert day and night to the prayers offered at this place. Believe me, I've chosen and sanctified this Temple that you have built: My Name is stamped on it forever; my eyes are on it and my heart in it always. As for you, if you live in my presence as your father David lived, pure in heart and action, living the life I've set out for you, attentively obedient to my guidance and judgments, then I'll back your kingly rule over Israel—make it a sure thing on a sure foundation. The same covenant guarantee I gave to David your father I'm giving to you, namely, 'You can count on always having a descendant on Israel's throne.' "But if you or your sons betray me, ignoring my guidance and judgments, taking up with alien gods by serving and worshiping them, then the guarantee is off: I'll wipe Israel right off the map and repudiate this Temple I've just sanctified to honor my Name. And Israel will be nothing but a bad joke among the peoples of the world. And this Temple, splendid as it now is, will become an object of contempt; tourists will shake their heads, saying, 'What happened here? What's the story behind these ruins?' Then they'll be told, 'The people who used to live here betrayed their God, the very God who rescued their ancestors from Egypt; they took up with alien gods, worshiping and serving them. That's what's behind this God-visited devastation.'" (2 Chronicles 7:12–22 MSG)

Solomon, David's son chosen by God to reign as king of Israel, prayed an incredible prayer of dedication (see 2 Chronicles 6). In his prayer he dedicated the newly built temple and prayed for the entire nation which included asking God to outline provisions for the people of the nation when they have turned away from Him and sinned.

Sometime later—perhaps months, possibly a few years—God responded to Solomon and told him that he had heard his prayer. God explained that if crisis comes to the nation as a result of the people having turned away from God and turning to their own wicked ways, then the first thing they must do is humble themselves. Then they must pray, seek the presence of the Lord, and finally turn from their sinful ways. As I have stated many times throughout this book, only God knows the heart of man. If our hearts are pure in the eyes of God, then true humility will show through. Our prayers become effectual and fervent. We will recognize there is no greater place of peace and protection than in the presence of the Lord, and no longer will our sinful will and ways be our lifestyle. These four steps of repentance and sorrow are guaranteed to get the attention of the almighty God. He will show forth his great grace and mercy on all who come to him in this manner, including an entire nation. Without humility, God does not even begin to look our way, and our prayers are a bunch of vain and empty words. However, when God sees our repentance is sincere and from our heart, only then will he listen from heaven, forgive our sins, and restore our land back to health (both personally and nationally). Not only will God restore the nation in crisis, but he promises to watch over and protect that nation and its people and respond to the nation's prayers as well. If the leaders of a nation pursue a lifestyle for God, God promises to support their leadership positions and make them successes in their roles as leaders.

Let me remind you that God is righteous and just. He keeps watch over the nation day and night, and he is sure to bring correction to the nation and its leaders if they choose to turn away and disobey the decrees and commands of God because of their pride. Pride is one of the chief culprits of one's downfall or failure. God brings down the proud but saves the humble (see Job 22:29). If you want favor with God, then humble yourself under the mighty hand of God by recognizing and expressing from your heart that you can do nothing without him and need him for all areas of your life. Humility is a place of lowliness from the heart. In no way does it mean that you are defeated and that others who do not embrace humility have an advantage over you. In fact, it actually means just the opposite. Those that are truly humble shall be exalted and honored.

By now you may have noticed that I continue to emphasize *true* humility? Could there possibly be such thing as false humility? Yes, absolutely! False humility seeks to hide itself under the pretense of humility. These people will assert just how humble they are. People who are truly humble do not recognize their humility because it is a natural condition emanating from their heart. Therefore, you likely will not hear them proclaim their humility. False humility is recognized when someone continuously announces they are humble, but they keep their self-ideas and self-motives in the forefront. These imitators of humility only believe in their own thoughts, plans, actions, and motives while everything and everyone else (including God) are secondary.

It is my prayer that the United States of America, the land of the free and the brave, founded on the principles of the almighty God, will humble themselves and pray, seek the wisdom of God, maintain his mighty name on the currency, restore prayer back into its schools, raise the banner above the banner, and never forget who has really kept and protected this nation. Are we a nation so proud of our accomplishments that we do not need God? Absolutely not! I call on every individual, community, city, and state of this great nation to take up a position of humility and give God all glory and honor, giving thanks to God for blessing our land and being the true keeper of our borders. Amen!

It is my prayer that all the great nations of this world (from the North America to Africa to Asia, from the Artic to the Antarctic, including every island of the seas) will humble themselves, pray, seek the presence of the almighty God, and turn from its wicked ways so that God may attend to their prayers, forgive their sins, and heal their land. Amen!

God is no respecter of persons, whether you are from a very poor and small village in the jungle or you lived your entire life in a royal palace with servants. God is Creator of every man, woman, and child, and his divine favor belongs to the humble. James 4:6 (NIV) says, "But he gives us more grace. That is why Scripture says: "God opposes the proud, but gives grace to the humble.""

God Blesses Those Who Are Humble

God blesses those who are humble, for they will inherit the whole earth (see Matthew 5:5 NLT). Jesus declared this himself when he gave his Sermon on the Mount. He opened the sermon with a list of kingdom character traits or attitudes (the Beatitudes) for living a Christlike lifestyle here on earth. The Beatitudes are our Christian code of conduct. They are key attitudes that followers of Christ must adapt in their hearts to truly live lives for Christ while on earth and receive kingdom rewards. The Beatitudes are in no way for picking and choosing which ones we can best handle. They are lifestyle values to be practiced as a whole.

For the sake of this chapter, we are going to analyze the attitude of humility and its significance. It is a weighty and must-have attitude God requires from us. In fact, as we learned from the previous Scripture, it is impossible for God to save us and heal us without us first humbling ourselves. In the Beatitudes, humility is listed twice—Matthew 5:3 and Matthew 5:5. For verse 3, most translations read, "Blessed are the poor in spirit." Who are the poor in spirit but those who are humbled and rate themselves insignificant? For verse 5, we will find that most translations read, "Blessed are the meek," while other translations may read, "Blessed are the humble or gentle; the ones who have not pride in their hearts." Humility, meekness, gentleness, and poor in spirit are all behavioral attitudes of lowliness. A lowly attitude is a humbled spirit. Most of society sees humility as a weakness in one's character, but God sees it as a character value of strength, and greatly rewards those who maintain humbled spirits.

The Attitude of Christ

Is there any encouragement from belonging to Christ? Any comfort from his love? Any fellowship together in the Spirit? Are your hearts tender and compassionate? Then make me truly happy by agreeing wholeheartedly with each other, loving one another, and working together with one mind and purpose. Don't be selfish; don't try to impress others. Be humble, thinking of others as better than yourselves. Don't look out only for your own interests, but take an interest in others, too. You must have the same attitude that Christ Jesus had. Though he was God, he did not think of equality with God as something to cling to. Instead, he gave up his divine privileges; he took the humble position of a slave and was born as a human being. When he appeared in human form, he humbled himself in obedience to God and died a criminal's death on a cross. Therefore, God elevated him to the place of highest honor and gave him the name above all other names, that at the name of Jesus every knee should bow, in heaven and on earth and under the earth, and every tongue confess that Jesus Christ is Lord, to the glory of God the Father. (Philippians 2:1–11 NLT)

Jesus Christ is our greatest example of humility. He existed in the beginning with God, and in fact, he was God (see John 1:1–2). But out of complete obedience to the will of God, he humbled himself and came to earth in the form of a mortal man (born of flesh and blood). Christ gave up his deity status and privileges and concerned himself with the will of God and the redemption of mankind back to the Father. Are you willing to serve others the way Christ serves? Are you willing to humble yourself and give up what you think are your rights or entitlements in order to serve and obey God, even if it means a complete change in your lifestyle? The thought of parting from your long-time and comfortable friend called "past lifestyle" may bring pain to your heart, tears to your eyes, and a sigh in your spirit, but I am here to confirm that the sacrifice is well worth the change.

When Jesus extended his hand to me, I felt the conviction in my heart and knew I could no longer hold on to my lifestyle at that time. In order to live virtuously for God, which was my heart's real desire, it was a necessity for me to humble myself and depart from my past sinful ways. All God needs is our broken spirit. Our broken and contrite heart (see Psalm 51:17) is the key to God's forgiveness of our past (sins) and redemption into a new hope and future with him. Matthew 23:12 reminds us that "those who exalt themselves will be humbled, and those who humble themselves will be exalted." When Christ humbled himself and obeyed, God exalted him in uncommon favor and honor, giving him the name above all other names.

Humility not only results in divine favor and honor but brings unity among individuals and organizations. In verses 1 through 4 of the previous text, the apostle Paul explains that a humbled mind-set promotes unity among people everywhere—at home, at the office, at church, and even among other leaders and nations. Diplomacy begins with a spirit of humility. Coming together with our hearts genuinely lowered (humbled) toward the care and well-being of others is a universal language well received by people of all nations. Without speaking a word, your humbled spirit will speak loud and clear. Humility opens the door for friendships and alliances to bud and blossom in due season. Humbled spirits allow both parties to begin with peaceful discussions on commonalities before they later move into tougher discussions and work out differences.

Resist Retaliation—Love Your enemies

In his Sermon on the Mount, Jesus Christ teaches us to resist retaliation and to love our enemies. This level of humility is sure to promote peaceful communities and nations.

> You have heard the law that says the punishment must match the injury: "An eye for an eye, and a tooth for a tooth." But I say, do not resist an evil person! If someone slaps you on the right cheek, offer the other cheek also. If you are sued in court and your shirt is taken from you, give your coat,

too. If a soldier demands that you carry his gear for a mile, carry it two miles. Give to those who ask, and don't turn away from those who want to borrow. You have heard the law that says, "Love your neighbor" and hate your enemy. But I say, love your enemies! Pray for those who persecute you! (Matthew 5:38–44 NLT)

In this world we live in, most people have the natural tendency to retaliate against those who have wronged them. In the previous Scripture, Jesus clearly teaches us to resist retaliation and to love our enemies. When someone says something bad or negative about us, we immediately look for ways to retaliate. Most of the time, we retaliate because of our own internal insecurities that provoke us to anger. Social media has become a major platform for verbal retaliation to rear its ugly head and feed the fire of pride that stirs within our sinful nature. Your pride says, "How dare you say those things about me! I'm the best, the greatest, the richest, the most famous, the smartest, etc."

So what does it take for people to resist retaliation and find it within their hearts to love their enemies? It takes *faith* in God through Jesus Christ, who laid down his life for us so that we no longer have to live according to this world. We can be transformed with renewed minds, humbled minds that seek to think like Christ. In Christ, our attitude and mind-set must change to that of living in God's kingdom. We must develop a great *trust* in God for his promised purpose for our lives and discount anything said to the contrary. In other words, "Know who you are, and who's you are!" By knowing who God, your Father, says you are, you are able to walk boldly and turn the other cheek.

Living Christlike

The very attitude of Christ is humility, so as we grow in Christ, we must also grow in humility, willing to sacrifice our own rights and privileges for the benefit of others.

Peter, one of Jesus's original twelve disciples, gave up his lifestyle and decided to follow Jesus. As Christ's follower and mentee, Peter received firsthand wisdom and knowledge from Jesus's teachings. Peter was given divine insight by the Holy Spirit and wholeheartedly confessed Jesus Christ as the promised Messiah (see Matthew 16:16). He genuinely demonstrated loyalty and faithfulness and became part of Jesus's inner circle. Although Peter shared a personal relationship with Jesus, he still maintained a hair-trigger attitude. His temper was one of immediate reaction to the slightest provocations. Needless to say, in his early days, humility and gentleness did not come naturally for Peter. As he matured in faith and became a true imitator of Christ, he learned tenderness and humility. Peter learned from Christ how to deal with provocations by turning the other cheek, how to handle those who did him wrong by having mercy on them, and even how to love and pray for his enemies. I pray that you will receive these words spoken by Peter encouraging us all to live holy for God:

> Finally, all of you should be of one mind. Sympathize with each other. Love each other as brothers and sisters. Be tenderhearted, and keep a humble attitude. Don't repay evil for evil. Don't retaliate with insults when people insult you. Instead, pay them back with a blessing. That is

what God has called you to do, and he will bless you for it. For the Scriptures say, "If you want to enjoy life and see many happy days, keep your tongue from speaking evil and your lips from telling lies. Turn away from evil and do good. Search for peace, and work to maintain it. The eyes of the Lord watch over those who do right, and his ears are open to their prayers. But the Lord turns his face against those who do evil." (1 Peter 3:8–12 NLT)

Godly Living

CHAPTER 10

Living Holy

Now if you obey me fully and keep my covenant, then out of all nations you will be my treasured possession. Although the whole earth is mine, you will be for me a kingdom of priests and a holy nation.

—Exodus 19:5–6 (NIV)

Living holy is not just a simple request but a command from God. It is a virtuous lifestyle that we must embrace in order to receive and experience the fullness of God and his promises for our lives. If we are going to walk in a covenant relationship with God, we must govern ourselves according to his commands and expectations. When God delivered the Israelites (his chosen people) out of Egypt (a place of bondage), he brought them to a place of rest and restoration at the base of Mount Sinai, where he spoke to them, giving detailed instructions and commandments on how to live their new lives. When he delivered them out of that place of bondage, God also had to deliver the bondage out of their hearts and minds by communicating his laws and instructions for living lives dedicated to him. There could be no more thinking and living like Egyptians. Their hearts and minds had to be transformed to live for their new Lord and Master, the almighty God, who rescued them from harsh slavery.

> Exactly two months after the Israelites left Egypt, they arrived in the wilderness of Sinai. After breaking camp at Rephidim, they came to the wilderness of Sinai and set up camp there at the base of Mount Sinai. Then Moses climbed the mountain to appear before God. The Lord called to him from the mountain and said, "Give these instructions to the family of Jacob; announce it to the descendants of Israel: 'You have seen what I did to the Egyptians. You know how I carried you on eagles' wings and brought you to myself. Now if you will obey me and keep my covenant, you will be my own special treasure from among all the peoples on earth; for all the earth belongs to me. And you will be my kingdom of priests, my holy nation.' This is the message you must give to the people of Israel." So Moses returned from the mountain and called together the elders of the people and told them everything the Lord had commanded him. And all the people responded together, "We will do everything the Lord has commanded." So Moses brought the people's answer back to the Lord. (Exodus 19:1–8 NLT)

A covenant relationship is a personal agreement between you and God. It is a promise that you will be faithful to him as he is faithful to you. In the previous passage, God proved his love and faithfulness by hearing the cries of the Israelite people and rescuing them from the oppression of the Egyptians. Today he is still that same loving and faithful God who hears the repentant cries of humanity, forgives them of their sins, and delivers them from their places of bondage, bringing them into new lives in Christ. Although we (humanity) are all created by God, God reserves special favor and privileges for those who are willing to trust him wholeheartedly and obey his voice—these faithful people God claims as his own special treasure, a holy nation, and a kingdom of priests who are set apart for his divine will, plan, and purpose.

As God's holy nation of people, we are commanded by God to live holy lives before him because he is holy. In Leviticus 19:2 (NLT), God commanded his people, "You must be holy because I, the Lord your God, am holy." God is faithful and deeply cares for his people. Therefore, he did not leave it up to his people to randomly guess what it meant to be holy. Instead he gave specific laws and instructions for living holy. Moses was God's chosen leader who not only led the Israelite people out of slavery but also taught and encouraged the nation to remain faithful to God's covenant with them. Through Moses, God delivered to the people his written Law, which included the Ten Commandments as well as a host of instructions on how to properly worship and live lives holy unto him (see Exodus 20 through 40 and the entire book of Leviticus).

God's Holiness

In the book of Numbers, God makes it clear that living holy is not about moral character from a human standard or perspective.

Living holy is about demonstrating God's holiness. So what is God's holiness, and how do we demonstrate it? Let's explore some key situations that occurred soon after the exodus as God sought to fulfill his promises to his people.

The Israelites encamped for two years at Mount Sinai before God gave their travel instructions (through Moses) to leave Mount Sinai and travel into the wilderness of Paran in order to move toward their Promised Land. As the Israelites approached their Promised Land, the Lord commanded Moses to send twelve leaders (the heads from each of Israel's twelve tribes) ahead to spy out and explore the land and the people of the land.

> After exploring the land for forty days, the men returned to Moses, Aaron, and the whole community of Israel at Kadesh in the wilderness of Paran. They reported to the whole community what they had seen and showed them the fruit they had taken from the land. This was their report to Moses: "We entered the land you sent us to explore, and it is indeed a bountiful country—a land flowing with milk and honey. Here is the kind of fruit it produces. But the people living there are powerful, and their towns are large and fortified. We even saw giants there, the descendants of Anak! The Amalekites live in the Negev, and the Hittites, Jebusites, and Amorites live in the hill country. The Canaanites live along the coast of the Mediterranean Sea and along the Jordan Valley." But Caleb tried to quiet the people as they stood before Moses. "Let's go at

once to take the land," he said. "We can certainly conquer it!" But the other men who had explored the land with him disagreed. "We can't go up against them! They are stronger than we are!" So they spread this bad report about the land among the Israelites: "The land we traveled through and explored will devour anyone who goes to live there. All the people we saw were huge. We even saw giants there, the descendants of Anak. Next to them we felt like grasshoppers, and that's what they thought, too!" (Numbers 13:25–33 NLT)

Upon their return, the leaders reported to Moses, Aaron, and the entire nation that the land was indeed a land flowing with milk and honey, but they quickly turned their positive report into a negative one by explaining that the cities were fortified and the people living there were strong and way too powerful for the Israelite nation to conquer. Caleb and Joshua, however, disagreed. By faith Caleb sought to silence the negative report with a can-do positive attitude. He believed and encouraged Moses and the entire nation to go immediately and take the land. Though most of the other leaders believed it to be impossible, Caleb believed that "with God, all things are possible" (see Matthew 19:26). From a human perspective, conquering the land was impossible, but from a faithful perspective that trusts in God, conquering the land was indeed possible. This is the same Promised Land that God promised to Abraham and his descendants. When God makes a promise, it is a sure thing, and he is looking for us to trust him during the journey. Because of the Israelites' lack of faith, which led to further rebellion and complaining, God condemned the people to wander for forty years in the wilderness.

In the first month of the year, the whole community of Israel arrived in the wilderness of Zin and camped at Kadesh. While they were there, Miriam died and was buried. There was no water for the people to drink at that place, so they rebelled against Moses and Aaron. The people blamed Moses and said, "If only we had died in the Lord's presence with our brothers! Why have you brought the congregation of the Lord's people into this wilderness to die, along with all our livestock? Why did you make us leave Egypt and bring us here to this terrible place? This land has no grain, no figs, no grapes, no pomegranates, and no water to drink!" Moses and Aaron turned away from the people and went to the entrance of the Tabernacle, where they fell face down on the ground. Then the glorious presence of the Lord appeared to them, and the Lord said to Moses, "You and Aaron must take the staff and assemble the entire community. As the people watch, speak to the rock over there, and it will pour out its water. You will provide enough water from the rock to satisfy the whole community and their livestock." So Moses did as he was told. He took the staff from the place where it was kept before the Lord. Then he and Aaron summoned the people to come and gather at the rock. "Listen, you rebels!" he shouted. "Must we bring you water from this rock?" Then Moses raised his hand and struck the rock twice with the staff, and water gushed out. So the entire community and their livestock drank their fill. But the Lord said to Moses and Aaron, "Because you did not trust me enough to demonstrate my holiness to the people of Israel, you will not lead them into the land I am giving them!" This place was known as the waters of Meribah (which means "arguing") because there the people of Israel argued with the Lord, and there he demonstrated his holiness among them. (Numbers 20:1–13 NLT)

After wandering for forty years in the wilderness, a new generation of Israelites were born and raised up while most of the original generation who had lived and come out of Egypt had died in the wilderness. Even this new generation lacked faith and soon forgot how God punished their parents for their unbelief and rebellion, and they, too, began to complain just as their parents did. Their lack of faith caused them to blame Moses and Aaron for all their troubles and discomforts instead of accepting responsibility for their own sinful ways and disobedience. Still today many people find it much easier to blame others for their troubles instead of accepting responsibility for their sinful lifestyles and disobedience. Sin separates us from God, and we find ourselves wandering for years before we come to the understanding that without God, it is impossible to know who we really are and who he purposed us to be. Until we put faith and trust in God, we will wander in the wilderness of darkness. Here's a word to the wise: A successful career is not a sign that you have found and mastered your purpose. Only through a faithful relationship with God that demonstrates his holiness will you arrive at your destiny and live out your true purpose.

The Israelite people severely nagged and complained to Moses and Aaron that there was no water to drink. Moses and Aaron then took the people's complaints before the Lord in prayer. Then God appeared to Moses and commanded him to take up his staff, which represented his God-given authority, and gather the community of people at the rock. In addition, God instructed Moses to speak to the rock in the sight of all the people, and when he spoke to the rock, God would then cause water to flow from it. Moses did as God asked and gathered the people at the rock, and in the sight of all the people, Moses raised his staff and struck the rock twice. Water then flowed abundantly from the rock, and the people as well as their livestock drank the water.

Although the Lord blessed his people with an abundant supply of water, he was displeased with Moses's actions. He said to Moses and Aaron, "Because you did not trust me enough to demonstrate my holiness to the people of Israel, you will not lead them into the land I am giving them" (see Numbers 20:12 NLT)! It displeased the Lord that Moses did not trust him and disobeyed his direct command. He commanded Moses to speak to the rock, but instead Moses struck the rock. It is imperative that we listen, trust, and obey the commands of God. Not long after they escaped from Egypt and entered the wilderness, the people complained of not having water to drink. At that particular time, God commanded Moses to strike the rock, and then water flowed from the rock. However, in this occurrence (almost forty years later), God clearly commanded Moses to speak to the rock.

Communing with God is a very important aspect of our relationship with him. Our dialogues with him are two-way.

When we speak, God listens and acts according to his will, and when God speaks, we must listen and obey his will. Just because God commands us to do something a particular way the first time, that does not mean if the situation arises again, we should do it the same as last time. This is the beauty of worshipping an all-knowing and omnipotent God. His strategies are perfect every time. God leads, and we follow. He speaks, and we hearken and obey his commands.

The Lord was displeased with Moses and Aaron's lack of trust and disobedience. In addition they displayed their lack of trust and disobedience in front of the entire congregation of people (the new generation of Israelite people who were already lacking in faith). As God's chosen leaders, Moses and Aaron had a huge responsibility, and that was to demonstrate before all the people that the Lord, their God, was (and still is) above all and should get all glory and honor. This kind of example or display of God's honor draws others closer to God, as they, too, will begin to believe and put their trust in him. Moses and Aaron's public display of disobedience did not demonstrate that God is exalted and worthy of complete devotion. Moses also took the credit for God's miracle of bringing water from the rock (see verse 10). Instead of publically displaying obedience and honor to God, Moses and Aaron publically displayed disobedience and dishonored God. Therefore, God's holiness was not demonstrated before the people.

Moses and Aaron's sinful actions did not go unpunished. The Lord then spoke to Moses and Aaron and informed them that they would not lead Israel into the Promised Land. Not only were they prohibited from leading the Israelite people into their

Promised Land, but they themselves would not get to cross over into the Promised Land. In the end, God received all honor and glory, and the Israelite people put their trust in the almighty God.

Because God is righteous and just, Moses and Aaron also suffered severe consequences for losing trust and rebelling against God. The consequences they suffered were just as severe as the consequences of the ten unbelieving Israelite leaders (all but Joshua and Caleb) who were sent to spy out the Promised Land. Their faith was shaken and as a result, they were prevented from moving forward. Consequently they missed out on the promises of God. By not demonstrating God's holiness, we, too will suffer consequences and miss out on God's promises.

As ambassadors for Christ, we are commanded to be holy, for the Lord, our God, is holy. We were created in the likeness of God's image for the purpose of reflecting God's image. By demonstrating God's holiness, naturally we will reflect God's image and remain holy to him. We demonstrate God's holiness when we let Jesus Christ reign in our hearts and lives as the exalted example for all to see, believe, and follow. All who choose to live for God demonstrate his holiness through their wholehearted *trust* in God, their *obedience* to God, their lifestyle of *humility*, their *love* for God and others, their *submission* to God's will, their *patience* to wait on God, and their *pure hearts*. People who live for God demonstrate his holiness in every area of their lives.

A Call to Live for God

This is a call to wholeheartedly worship and live a holy life for God. God is calling us back to the ground-level character values he taught us from the beginning—character values that must be working within us in order to wholeheartedly serve him. With these seven principles implemented in our lives, we are sure to live virtuously for God.

> Then Jesus said to his disciples, "If any of you wants to be my follower, you must turn from your selfish ways, take up your cross, and follow me. If you try to hang on to your life, you will lose it. But if you give up your life for my sake, you will save it. And what do you benefit if you gain the whole world but lose your own soul? Is anything worth more than your soul? For the Son of Man will come with his angels in the glory of his Father and will judge all people according to their deeds. (Matthew 16:24–27 NLT)

www.ingramcontent.com/pod-product-compliance
Lightning Source LLC
Chambersburg PA
CBHW021526150726
47990CB00006B/2118